500 CHAIRS

D1465176

500 CHAIRS

CELEBRATING TRADITIONAL AND INNOVATIVE DESIGNS

LARK CRAFTS

Asheville

SENIOR EDITOR: **Ray Hemachandra**

EDITOR: **Larry Shea**

DEVELOPMENTAL EDITOR: **James Knight**

ART DIRECTOR: **Jackie Kerr**

COVER DESIGNER: **Cindy LaBreacht**

PROOFREADER: **Mark Bloom**

FRONT COVER
John Makepeace
Trine, 1998

BACK COVER, FROM TOP LEFT
David P. Barresi
Rocking/Arm Chair, 2003

Mordechai Schleifer
Couch of Court Peacocks Tail, 2001

John Makepeace
Sylvan, 1980s

Larry Fagan and Carolyn Schmitz
Striped Lounge, 2005

Michael Fortune
Untitled, 2006

SPINE
Jacque Allen
Iron Ladder Back Chair, 2005

FRONT FLAP, FROM TOP
Jacque Allen
Red Rebar Chair, 2006

Isaac Arms
Steel Rocker, 2004

BACK FLAP
Judy Kensley McKie
Monkey Chair, 1994

PAGE 3
Mordechai Schleifer
The Oracles' Arm Chair, 2001

PAGE 5
Michael Gloor
Window Chair I, 2002

LARK CRAFTS

An Imprint of Sterling Publishing
387 Park Avenue South
New York, NY 10016

If you have questions or comments about
this book, please visit: larkcrafts.com

Library of Congress Cataloging-in-Publication Data

500 chairs : celebrating traditional and innovative designs / Ray
Hemachandra, editor.
     p. cm.
  title: Five hundred chairs
  Includes index.
  ISBN-13: 978-1-57990-872-0 (pb-trade pbk. : alk. paper)
  ISBN-10: 1-57990-872-1 (pb-trade pbk. : alk. paper)
  1. Furniture making. 2. Chairs. I. Hemachandra, Ray. II. Title: Five
hundred chairs.
  TT197.5.C45A185 2008
  684.1'3—dc22

                                      2007043325

1 0 9 8 7 6 5 4 3

Published by Lark Crafts
An Imprint of Sterling Publishing Co., Inc.
387 Park Avenue South, New York, NY 10016

Text © 2008, Lark Crafts, an Imprint of Sterling Publishing Co., Inc.
Photography © 2008, Artist/Photographer

Distributed in Canada by Sterling Publishing,
c/o Canadian Manda Group, 165 Dufferin Street
Toronto, Ontario, Canada M6K 3H6

Distributed in the United Kingdom by GMC Distribution Services,
Castle Place, 166 High Street, Lewes, East Sussex, England BN7 1XU

Distributed in Australia by Capricorn Link (Australia) Pty Ltd.,
P.O. Box 704, Windsor, NSW 2756 Australia

Manufactured in China

ISBN 13: 978-1-57990-872-0

For information about custom editions, special sales, and premium and corporate
purchases, please contact Sterling Special Sales Department at 800-805-5489
or specialsales@sterlingpub.com.

Requests for information about desk and examination copies available to college and
university professors must be submitted to academic@larkbooks.com. Our complete
policy can be found at www.larkcrafts.com.

Contents

Introduction

Tom Loeser
Forest Furniture | 2004

"Sometimes a chair is just a chair." While it may be tempting to swap *chair* for *cigar* in the quotation famously attributed to Sigmund Freud, this aphorism is true for few, if any, of the 500 chairs presented in this book. A chair, like Freud's cigar, is metaphorically loaded.

This is partly because of the chair's intimate relationship with the human body. Even the names of its parts—legs, seat, back, arms—describe the human form. A chair not only supports its occupant in work or in leisure, but it also ornaments, conveys status, and links the person seated to the history of objects and culture. Chairs once were reserved for a select few: chieftains, pharaohs, potentates. The throne was the symbol of their power. To this day we refer to the leader of an organization or committee as the *chairperson*, or more recently as simply the *chair*.

Today, chairs are so ubiquitous that they are sometimes used by artists and philosophers to represent mundane or generic objects. Several artists represented in this book have distilled their chairs to the point that they become a symbol or shorthand for chairs and the associations they invoke, such as that of human presence, absence, or both. See, for example, how Jennifer Anderson's "Conversation" (page 27) and Matthias Pliessnig's "Bends" (page 39) play with negative spaces to comment on the act of sitting itself.

Some chairs are built for comfort, like a leisurely ride in a sleek Sam Maloof rocker (page 121), and others for speed, like a café chair whose austere design encourages the patron not to linger over her latte too long. Chairs, like Archie Bunker's tattered old easy chair, can create a sense of security and belonging. While we all have sat in chairs that were unintentionally punitive, some are deliberately so. Take, for example, the state of Alabama's infamous death-row chair "Yellow Mama," or, for a much subtler sense of discomfort, imagine sitting in Gord Peteran's claustrophobic "Ark" (page 148).

Garry Knox Bennett
Great Granny Rietveld | 2003

Judy Kensley McKie
Seagull Chair | 1999

Chairs, notoriously difficult to design and make, tend to be the works for which furniture designers and makers are remembered. As a furniture artist myself, I know what a challenge it is to work out all the visual and spatial elements required to make a chair look right from all angles, and still mesh gracefully with the human body, in all its sizes and forms. I once was with a large group of furniture makers touring the great American architect Frank Lloyd Wright's Arizona compound, Taliesin West, where we were all allowed to sit in Wright-designed chairs. The tour guide asked, "Are those chairs comfortable?" The verdict was an immediate and unanimous "NO!"

Bruce Metcalf, a frequent writer on the subject of craft, has suggested that furniture tends to be evolutionary rather than revolutionary. Many of the chairmakers featured here proudly take their place at the end of generation upon generation of master artisans. Using traditional hand tools, Curtis

Buchanan (pages 338 and 358) makes incremental elaborations on the Windsor style, while Brian Boggs brings an elegant refinement to the ladderback chair that makes this traditional form seem contemporary.

Other artists seek to break from tradition and play with it at the same time. Furniture about furniture, what I think of as *metafurniture*, is Tom Loeser's forte. His chairs question how chairs function and how we interact with them. The quintessentially irreverent Garry Knox Bennett skewers and lovingly roasts modernist icons in a recent series of chairs that includes "Great Granny Rietveld," while Jake Cress directs a dignified Chippendale side chair in a goofy slapstick (page 373).

Some chairs start with the question, "What if?"—the most familiar such question in my own work being "What if a chair were made from garden vegetables?" By asking questions like this, artists sometimes develop a personal imagery or visual vocabulary that plays an important role in their work. Stylized animal forms enliven Judy Kensley McKie's chairs, and the chip-carved embellishments in Kristina Madsen's chairs (pages 242, 243, and 374) suggest the intricacy and transparency of lace and needlework. Theatricality has its place as well. In a gentle act of "chairorism" that would occur only to a furniture maker, Michael Hosaluk did his final glue-up of some of his chairs around tree trunks and other objects in the streetscape (page 261).

Brian Boggs
Untitled | 2006

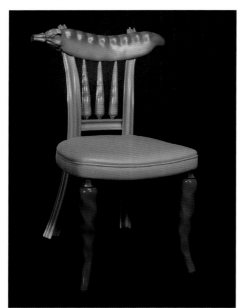

Craig Nutt
Celery Chair with Peppers,
Carrots & Snow Peas | 2005

The chairs in this book are made from a wide variety of materials, including wood, metal, clay, glass, concrete, fiberglass, and industrial felt. The work of emerging artists appears alongside chairs by many of the masters of contemporary studio furniture. Also included are some miniature and sculptural chairs by artists who normally are not associated with the studio-furniture field. The work ranges from rustic to refined, traditional to futuristic, and absurd to sublime. This book is filled with superb chairs, engaging ideas, and good humor, and I hope you find investigating these chairs to be as stimulating and enjoyable as I have.

Craig Nutt, Juror

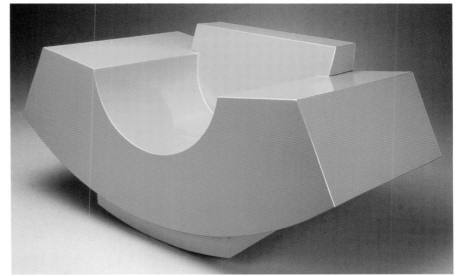

THE CHAIRS

David Upfill-Brown

Amatory Chair | 2006

30 X 28 X 19 INCHES (75 X 71 X 48 CM)
Cherry, leather
PHOTO BY JIM DUGAN

Judy Kensley McKie

Monkey Chair | 1994

36 X 25 X 25 INCHES (90 X 64 X 64 CM)
Walnut, bronze
PHOTOS BY SCOTT MCCUE

John Makepeace

Vine | 1994

33 X 20 X 20 INCHES (83 X 51 X 51 CM)

Limewood

PHOTO BY ARTIST

This garden chair has a dual-themed mosaic of nature and urban living and was inspired by the humor and dark whimsy of children's artwork. CONNIE LEVATHES

Connie Levathes

Untitled | 2007

43 X 39 X 27 INCHES (108 X 98 X 69 CM)
Glass tile mosaic, recycled styrofoam, cement, fiberglass mesh
PHOTOS BY DANA DAVIS

Charles B. Cobb
Sculptchair #1, #3, #2 | 1999

EACH: 5 X 3 X 3 INCHES (13 X 8 X 8 CM)
Wenge, maple, fabric
PHOTO BY HAP SAKWA

Robb Helmkamp

Lotus Meditation Chair | 2006

20 X 30 X 28 INCHES (50 X 75 X 71 CM)
Walnut, maple, laminated door skins
PHOTOS BY ARTIST

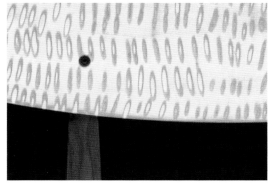

Jon Brooks

Peony | 1997

72 X 28 X 24 INCHES (180 X 70 X 60 CM)

Walnut, maple, color pencil, lacquer, acrylic, varnish

PHOTO BY DEAN POWELL

Richard Jacobus

Between a Rock and a Hard Place | 2006

57 X 16 X 16 INCHES (143 X 41 X 41 CM)

Steel, copper, brass

PHOTO BY JIM CHESTNUT

Jacque Allen

Red Rebar Chair | 2006

48 X 19 X 17 INCHES (120 X 46 X 43 CM)

Birch, buffalo hide, rebar steel and tie wire, paint

PHOTOS BY ARTIST

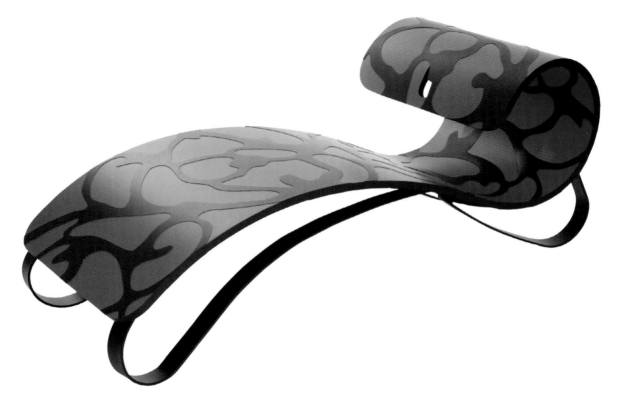

Ruth Fore

Vroom | 2006

26 X 22 X 36 INCHES (66 X 56 X 90 CM)

Plywood, steel

PHOTO BY TUAN NYUGEN

This chair is composed of six rolls of interwoven felt, pressed together with stainless steel fasteners. The soft chair changes through use, like a leather shoe that is broken in over time.

LOTHAR WINDELS

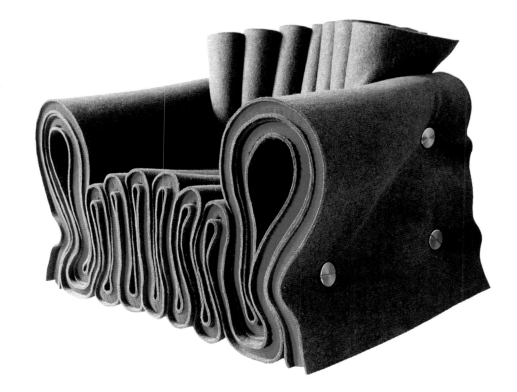

Lothar Windels

Joseph Felt Chair | 2000

32 X 44 X 36 INCHES (80 X 110 X 90 CM)
Stainless steel, wool felt
PHOTO BY ARTIST

Curtis K. LaFollette

1216/63 | 2005

33 X 24 X 36 INCHES (83 X 58 X 90 CM)
Steel rod frame, chrome steel, fabric
PHOTO BY NASH STUDIO

Jeff Michael Weathers

Reading Chair #3 | 2007

32 X 29 X 36 INCHES (80 X 73 X 90 CM)

Maple

PHOTO BY ARTIST

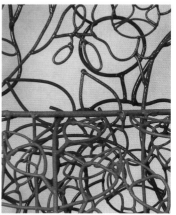

Megan Auman

Chair (From Living Room) | 2006

35 X 23 X 27 INCHES (88 X 58 X 69 CM)

Powder-coated steel

PHOTOS BY ARTIST

Clear Inc.

Vine Chair | 2006

36 X 21 X 35 INCHES (90 X 53 X 88 CM)
Grape vines, resin
PHOTO BY O'TYSON PHOTOGRAPHY

This chaise was the first piece in a collection entitled A Few Essential Pieces of Furniture.
Each piece multitasks and is designed to suit the small spaces of New York City living. DANIEL KOPEC

Daniel Kopec
Chaise | 2003

24 X 24 X 68 INCHES (61 X 61 X 170 CM)
Stainless steel, wool upholstery
PHOTOS BY DAVID WILLIAMS

Susan R. Ewing

Serie Arquitectonica: Folded Chair II | 2001

44 X 22 X 20 INCHES (110 X 56 X 50 CM)

Aircraft aluminum

PHOTO BY JEFFREY SABO

25

Po Shun Leong

Silhouette Chair | 2007

EACH: 36 X 18 X 20 INCHES (90 X 46 X 51 CM)
Ebonized ash, painted polypropylene
PHOTO BY ARTIST

This chair is meant to be slightly uncomfortable. My hope is that users will move around in an attempt to "fit," ultimately finding themselves in positions and postures that are not their own. JENNIFER ANDERSON

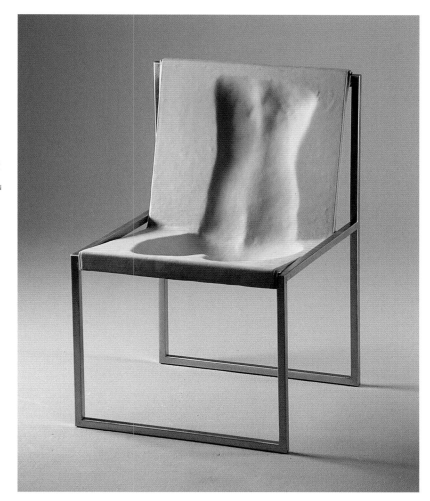

Jennifer Anderson
Conversation | 2006

30 X 20 X 19 INCHES (75 X 51 X 48 CM)
Stainless steel, fiberglass, leather
PHOTO BY LARRY STANLEY

Hank Holzer

Hip Hobbit Chair | 2007

CHAIR: 37 X 15 X 20 INCHES (93 X 38 X 51 CM)
Elm, wenge
PHOTO BY ARTIST

Sam Batchelor
Untitled | 2007

36 X 13 X 23 INCHES (90 X 33 X 58 CM)
Honduras mahogany, steel
PHOTOS BY ARTIST

Tony Kenway

Rocker | 2000

35 X 24 X 35 INCHES (88 X 61 X 88 CM)

Quilted Tasmanian blackwood

PHOTO BY DAVID YOUNG

David P. Barresi

Rocking/Arm Chair | 2003

36 X 56 X 48 INCHES (90 X 140 X 120 CM)

Ash, leather

PHOTO BY DIETRICH FLOETER

Benjamin Strear

Cantilever Rocker | 2005

30 X 17 X 60 INCHES (75 X 43 X 150 CM)

White oak

PHOTO BY MARK JOHNSTON

David O. Wade
Untitled | 2006

48 X 24 X 48 INCHES (120 X 60 X 120 CM)
Pomelle sapele, curly maple
PHOTO BY ARTIST

Charles Sthreshley
Crete Seat 2 | 2000

49 X 31 X 29 INCHES (123 X 78 X 72 CM)
Concrete, rope
PHOTO BY ARTIST

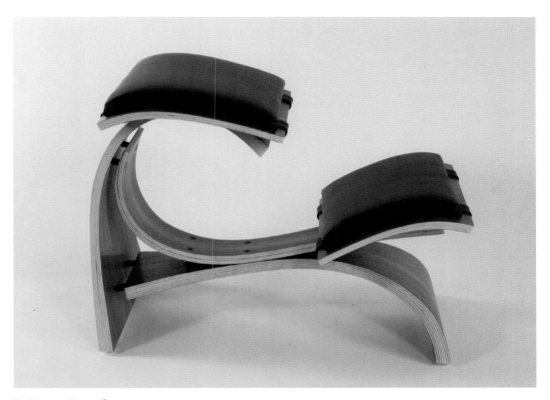

Tatiana Tessel

Balance Chair | 2004

18 X 18 X 27 INCHES (46 X 46 X 69 CM)

Poplar, black walnut, commercial veneers, steel, leather

PHOTO BY ARTIST

Daniella Peña

Mecedora | 2006

28 X 32 X 35 INCHES (71 X 80 X 88 CM)
Stainless steel, cotton rope
PHOTOS BY ARTIST

Luce Robineau

Queenie | 2001

56 X 35 X 28 INCHES (140 X 88 X 70 CM)

Poplar, willow

PHOTO BY PAUL SIMON

Clifton Monteith
Idaho Club Chair | 2005

36 X 30 X 30 INCHES (90 X 75 X 75 CM)
Willow, aspen
PHOTOS BY JOHN WILLIAMS

Alan Bradstreet
Willow Chair | 2001

53 X 33 X 30 INCHES (133 X 83 X 75 CM)
Willow, aspen
PHOTO BY DENNIS GRIGGS

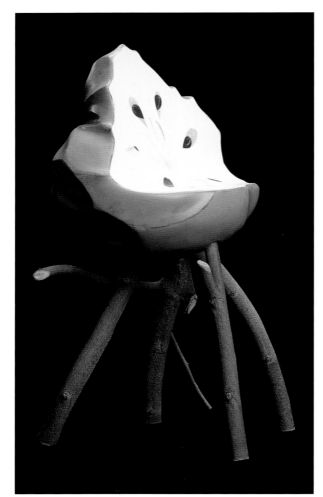

Margaret Matson

Cherimoya | 1998

12 X 7 X 7 INCHES (31 X 18 X 18 CM)

Basswood, cherimoya branches, paint

PHOTOS BY SCOTT MCCLAINE

"Bends" appears to be squeezing and compressing to support a person who isn't there. I think of it as a soft grid of wood being formed by the sitter's weight. I took the moment of reaction and froze it. MATTHIAS PLIESSNIG

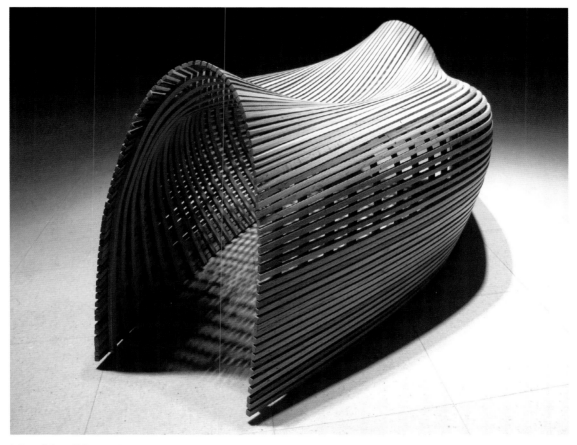

Matthias Pliessnig
Bends | 2006

30 X 44 X 28 INCHES (75 X 110 X 70 CM)
Steam bent oak
PHOTO BY ARTIST

"Green Treen" is a modern style of rustic furniture, combining "treen," an Old English word meaning directly from the tree, and "green," using sustainable, recycled, or invasive tree species for construction materials.

PAUL RUHLMANN

Paul Ruhlmann

Green Treen Chair | 1999

40 X 22 X 19 INCHES (100 X 56 X 48 CM)
Red maple saplings, walnut, Shaker tape
PHOTO BY ARTIST

Roger Hauge
Rosemarie Hohol
McIntosh | 1998

38 X 21 X 20 INCHES (95 X 53 X 51 CM)
Peeled and dyed maple, hand-woven cotton
PHOTO BY ROGER HAUGE

Sue Roberts
Spiral Back Chair | 1999

46 X 27 X 20 INCHES (115 X 66 X 50 CM)
Marine plywood, fir, acrylic paint
PHOTO BY ARTIST

Rhea Giffin

Dali's Darlin' Ziraffe | 2005

56 X 32 X 26 INCHES (140 X 80 X 65 CM)

Wood chair, cellulose insulation, wheat paste,
paper, plaster cloth, insulation foam,
acrylic paint, polyurethane

PHOTOS BY S. JOSEPH SHARNETSKY

Sabiha Mujtaba
Naga II | 2004

41 X 24 X 25 INCHES (103 X 62 X 64 CM)
Black limba, curly maple
PHOTOS BY BART KASTEN

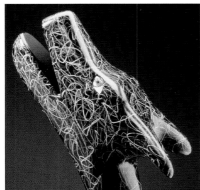

Jon Brooks
One Voice | 1998

64 X 45 X 45 INCHES (160 X 113 X 113 CM)
Maple, acrylic, lacquer, varnish
PHOTOS BY DEAN POWELL

Dale Lewis

Seahorsing Around | 2004

71 X 38 X 27 INCHES (178 X 95 X 69 CM)

Dyed and natural cherry, maple, sycamore

PHOTO BY RALPH ANDERSON

Jennifer Schwarz
Salmon Seat | 1996

39 X 53 X 18 INCHES (98 X 132 X 45 CM)
Maple, cherry, upholstery
PHOTO BY GREGG KROGSTAD

Judy Kensley McKie

Bird Chair | 1997

39 X 20 X 27 INCHES
(99 X 51 X 69 CM)

Alaskan cedar

PHOTOS BY GREG HEINS

Judy Kensley McKie
Seagull Chair | 1999

40 X 33 X 27 INCHES (100 X 83 X 69 CM)
Cast bronze
PHOTO BY SCOTT MCCUE

Pegasus combines all of my fantasies about wings, wheels, and torsion bar suspensions. DAVID M. GROSZ

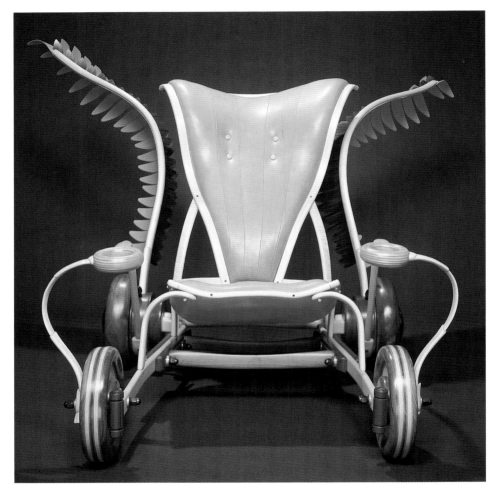

David M. Grosz

Pegasus | 1975

70 X 85 X 86 INCHES (175 X 213 X 215 CM)
Solid wood, deerskin, metals
PHOTOS BY ARTIST

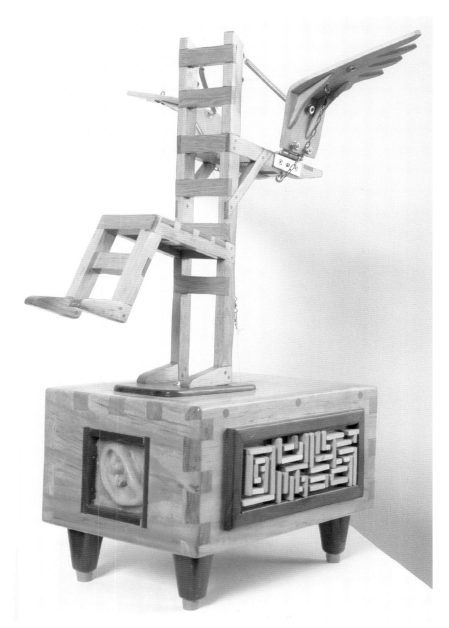

Rob Millard-Mendez

Icarus Chair | 2004

14 X 10 X 20 INCHES (36 X 25 X 51 CM)

Wood, steel, wax

PHOTO BY JOHN MACIEL

Thomas R. Wargin
Untitled | 2005

19 X 21 X 46 INCHES (48 X 53 X 115 CM)
Cherry, aluminum, glass
PHOTO BY WILLIAM LEMKE

Richard Bronk

Untitled | 1995

51 X 24 X 23 INCHES (128 X 61 X 58 CM)

Walnut, curly maple, African porcupine quill

PHOTO BY BILL LEMKE

Jeff Stockham

Spring Chair | 2002

41 X 24 X 52 INCHES (103 X 61 X 130 CM)

Maple

PHOTO BY IAN DEA

Lewis Irving

Untitled | 2006

31 X 24 X 27 INCHES (78 X 61 X 69 CM)

Ash, steel, lacquer, hardware

PHOTO BY ARTIST

David P. Barresi

Adirondack Style Chair | 2003

36 X 40 X 40 INCHES (90 X 100 X 100 CM)

Ash

PHOTO BY DIETRICH FLOETER

Curtis Minier

Dining Chair | 2005

31 X 24 X 22 INCHES (78 X 60 X 55 CM)
Walnut, bubinga, bronzed steel, leather

PHOTOS BY HARVEY BERGMAN

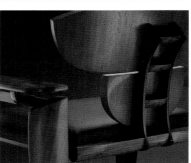

Andrew Muggleton

Balustrade Chaise | 2003

31 X 20 X 59 INCHES (78 X 51 X 148 CM)

Wenge, mahogany, aluminum rails, suede

PHOTO BY DEAN POWELL

Marcus Papay

Catapult | 2007

16 X 48 X 20 INCHES (41 X 120 X 51 CM)
Ash, steel cable, steel sheet

PHOTOS BY LARRY STANLEY

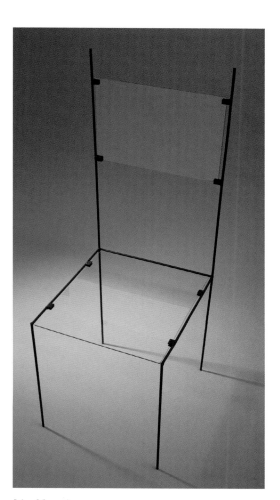

Liz Kerrigan
After You (No. 1) | 2007

40 X 15 X 16 INCHES (100 X 38 X 41 CM)
Steel, plate glass
PHOTO BY JOSEPH SAVANT

Jacque Allen
Iron Ladder Back Chair | 2005

58 X 19 X 19 INCHES (145 X 48 X 48 CM)
Cherry, buffalo hide, iron, copper rivets
PHOTO BY ARTIST

Andy Buck

Lounge Lizard Chairs | 2000

EACH: 34 X 19 X 26 INCHES (85 X 48 X 66 CM)

Ebonized mahogany, fabric

PHOTO BY BILL BACHHUBER

Libby Schrum

A Single Black Line | 2005

38 X 19 X 55 INCHES (95 X 48 X 138 CM)

Maple, leather

PHOTO BY JIM DUGAN

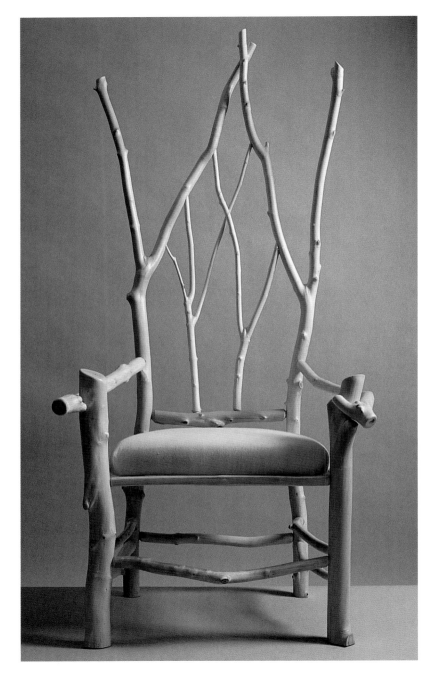

Daniel Mack

Peeled Fork Chair | 1993

50 X 24 X 24 INCHES (125 X 61 X 61 CM)

Peeled maple

PHOTO BY BOBBY HANSSON

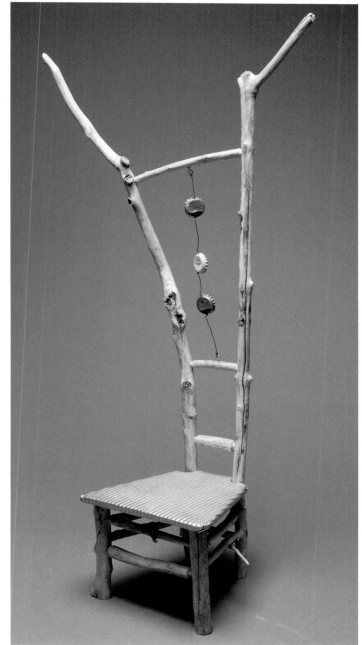

I remember pulling the cork off the inside of bottle tops as a child. The tops here still have the cork intact and were found hidden away in an abandoned store's bottle opener.
AMY LANSBURG

Amy Lansburg
Pop Art | 2006

8 X 8 X 31 INCHES (20 X 20 X 78 CM)
Lake Superior driftwood, vintage pop tops
PHOTO BY JAMIE HARMON

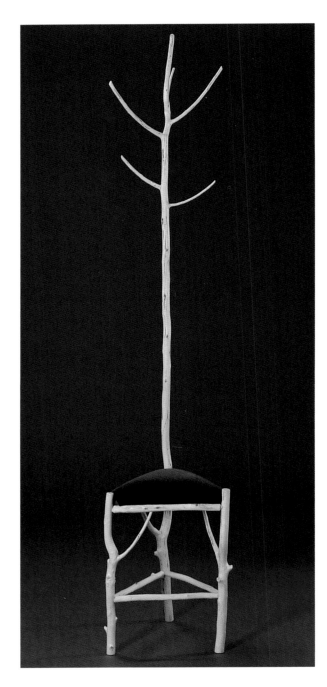

Alan Bradstreet

Valet | 1998

75 X 14 X 18 INCHES (188 X 36 X 46 CM)

Poplar, upholstery

PHOTO BY DENNIS GRIGGS

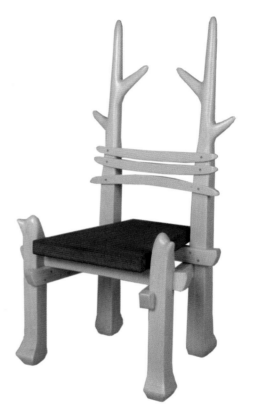

Carol Russell
Sticks and Stone Chair | 2007

48 X 25 X 21 INCHES (120 X 64 X 53 CM)
Basswood, basalt
PHOTO BY ROSS HILMOE

Chris Martin
Katai Chair II | 2002

EACH: 63 X 22 X 24 INCHES (158 X 56 X 61 CM)
Cherry, steel
PHOTO BY GEORGE ENSLEY

Daniel Mack

Green Man Chair | 2003

58 X 26 X 24 INCHES (145 X 66 X 61 CM)
Wood, natural materials
PHOTO BY ADAM KURTZ

John Makepeace

Sylvan | 1980s

EACH: 36 X 23 X 22 INCHES (90 X 58 X 56 CM)

Washed English oak

PHOTO BY ARTIST

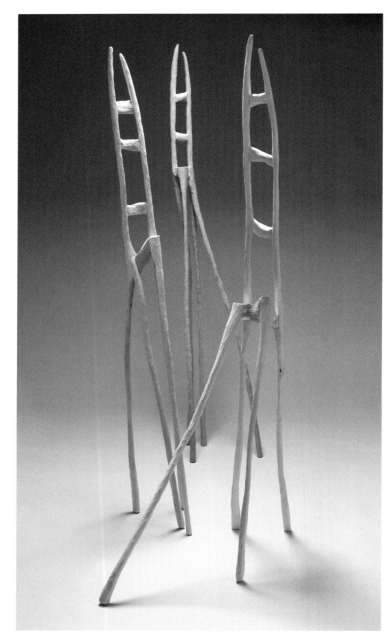

Chris M. Todd

Tripartite | 2006

71 X 24 X 88 INCHES (180 X 61 X 224 CM)

Basswood

PHOTO BY EDEN REINER

Chris Martin
Tsuba Chair | 2005

EACH: 62 X 27 X 19 INCHES (155 X 69 X 48 CM)
Chechen, bronze, steel
PHOTO BY GEORGE ENSLEY

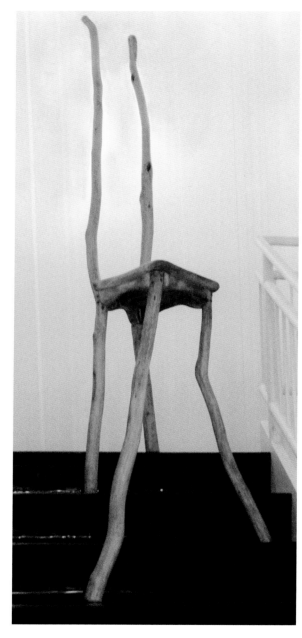

Chris M. Todd

Stare Chair | 2006

96 X 27 X 30 INCHES (240 X 69 X 75 CM)

Birch saplings, basswood

PHOTO BY EDEN REINER

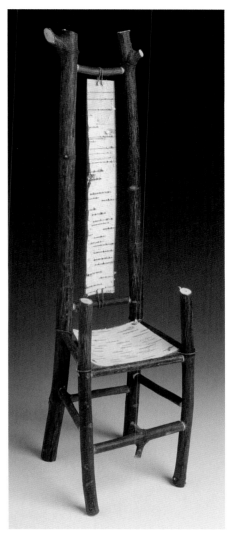

JoAnne Russo
Twig Chair | 2006

18 X 5 X 5 INCHES (46 X 13 X 13 CM)
Striped maple, birch bark, waxed linen
PHOTO BY JEFF BAIRD

Tom Loeser
Forest Furniture | 2004

74 X 20 X 22 INCHES (185 X 51 X 56 CM)
Acacia, existing tree
PHOTO BY ARTIST

A vineyard has given me its oak wine barrels, and I am interested in creating furniture from them instead of having them cut in half and turned into yet more planters. The natural curve of the barrel staves is what attracted me to the project, and it is a constant challenge. The wonderful color of the wine-soaked interior is an additional treat.

KERRY MARSHALL

Kerry Marshall
Bordeaux Chair | 2006

36 X 20 X 24 INCHES (90 X 50 X 60 CM)
Recycled white oak wine barrel staves
PHOTO BY ARTIST

John Grew Sheridan

"1 x 2" Pine Slat Chair | 1996

36 X 20 X 24 INCHES (90 X 50 X 60 CM)

Pine

PHOTO BY JOE SCHOPPLEIN

Jeff Soderbergh

Grande Lounge | 2001

48 X 60 X 11 INCHES (120 X 150 X 28 CM)

1902 Kimball Baby Grand piano,
oak Empire chair leg circa 1830,
walnut, velvet

PHOTO BY DAVE HANSEN

Matthew E. Nauman

Adirondack | 2005

42 X 24 X 24 INCHES (105 X 60 X 60 CM)

Red oak, sassafras

PHOTO BY ROY ENGELBRECHT

Rebecca Cook

Hickory and Steel Rocking Chair | 2004

50 X 23 X 50 INCHES (125 X 58 X 125 CM)

Hickory veneer, poplar, steel

PHOTO BY JOHN STAMETS

Greg Gehner

Blocky | 2007

29 X 16 X 20 INCHES (73 X 41 X 51 CM)

Cherry, steel

PHOTO BY ARTIST

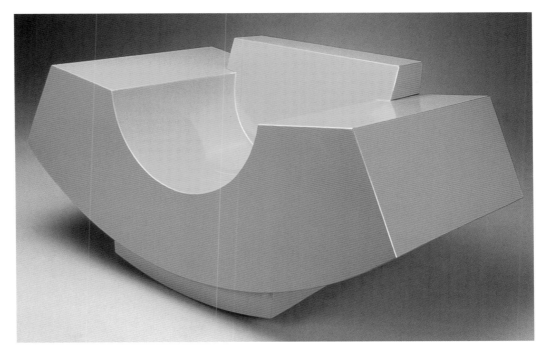

Isaac Arms

Steel Rocker | 2004

31 X 60 X 30 INCHES (78 X 150 X 75 CM)

Steel, powder coating

PHOTO BY BILL LEMKE

Judiyaba
Rufus Olivier

Opus 00 | 2005

49 X 11 X 24 INCHES (123 X 28 X 60 CM)
Wood, acrylic and latex paint
PHOTOS BY KRISTIN HALGEDAHL

Susan Borger

*Caterpillar Concentrics
with Fringe* | 2007

34 X 19 X 14 INCHES (85 X 48 X 36 CM)
Reclaimed chair, cotton fabrics

PHOTO BY ARTIST

Hugh Montgomery

Eagle Harbor Bar Chair | 2007

EACH: 34 X 27 X 21 INCHES (85 X 68 X 53 CM)

Maple

PHOTO BY ART GRICE

David Upfill-Brown

Conversation Piece | 1995

28 X 48 X 20 INCHES (71 X 120 X 51 CM)
Queensland silver ash, microsuede
PHOTO BY ANDREW SIKORSKI / ART ATELIER

Wharton Esherick (1887–1970)
IS WIDELY CONSIDERED THE FATHER
OF CONTEMPORARY STUDIO FURNITURE
MAKERS. A PAINTER AND SCULPTOR, HE
INITIALLY STARTED MAKING FURNITURE
TO FURNISH HIS OWN HOME, AND LATER,
FOR ARTISTIC EXPRESSION AND FOR SALE.
HIS INDIVIDUALISTIC, OFTEN ECCENTRIC,
FURNITURE INSPIRED A GENERATION OF
YOUNG FURNITURE MAKERS WHO WENT
ON TO TEACH SCORES OF OTHERS. THE
WHARTON ESHERICK MUSEUM IN PAOLI,
PENNSYLVANIA, HOUSES A COLLECTION
OF HIS WORK IN HIS HOME AND STUDIO,
A WORK OF ART IN ITSELF. THE MUSEUM
IS OPEN BY APPOINTMENT.

Wharton Esherick
Wagon Wheel Chair | 1931

40 X 25 X 24 INCHES (100 X 64 X 61 CM)
Ash, hickory fellows and shafts, harness leather

PHOTO BY MANSFIELD BASCOM
COURTESY OF WHARTON ESHERICK MUSEUM, PA

Wharton Esherick

SK Chair | 1942

30 X 20 X 23 INCHES (75 X 51 X 58 CM)

Walnut, fabric

PHOTO BY MANSFIELD BASCOM
COURTESY OF WHARTON ESCHERICK MUSEUM, PA

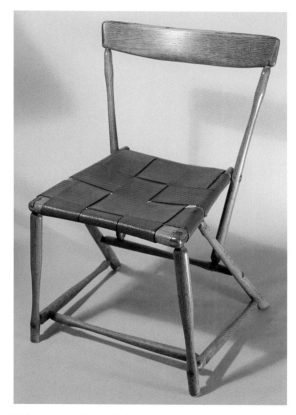

Wharton Esherick

Hammer Handle Chair | 1938

31 X 21 X 22 INCHES (78 X 53 X 56 CM)

Hickory, ash, canvas, paint

PHOTO BY MANSFIELD BASCOM
COURTESY OF WHARTON ESCHERICK MUSEUM, PA

Jere Osgood
Dining or Desk Chair | 2006
36 X 17 X 19 INCHES (90 X 43 X 48 CM)
Cherry, antelope leather
PHOTO BY BILL TRUSLOW

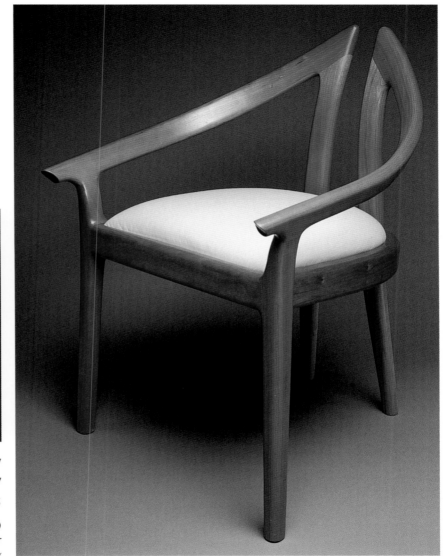

Larry Buechley
Nancy Buechley
Alpha Chair | 2005

32 X 23 X 23 (80 X 58 X 58 CM)
Cherry, leather
PHOTOS BY ADDISON DOTY

Tim Hintz

Child's High Chair | 2006

36 X 20 X 20 INCHES (90 X 50 X 50 CM)
Red oak, hickory bark
PHOTO BY JOHN LUCAS

Seth Rolland

Finback Stool | 2005

41 X 18 X 16 INCHES (103 X 46 X 40 CM)
Cherry
PHOTO BY FRANK ROSS

R.A. Laufer
Split-Back Counter Chair | 2007

37 X 20 X 23 INCHES (93 X 51 X 58 CM)
Cherry
PHOTOS BY BOB BARRETT

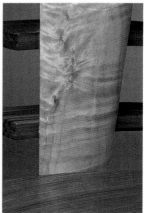

Seth Rolland

Trimerous Chair | 2003

32 X 27 X 24 INCHES (80 X 68 X 61 CM)

Walnut, curly maple, sapele veneer

PHOTOS BY PAT POLLARD

Michael Oleson

Wedge Chairs | 2003

EACH: 52 X 18 X 22 INCHES (130 X 46 X 56 CM)

Poplar

PHOTOS BY ARTIST

Robert Griffith

Dining Chair | 2005

34 X 22 X 23 INCHES (85 X 56 X 58 CM)

Steel, fabric

PHOTO BY LISA HINKLE

David Upfill-Brown

Pair of Chair | 1988

EACH: 30 X 26 X 20 INCHES (75 X 66 X 51 CM)

Jarrah, silk

PHOTO BY ARTIST

Rachel Avivi
Pair Chair | 2007

39 X 60 X 25 INCHES (98 X 150 X 63 CM)
Walnut, wood backrests, oil paint
PHOTO BY REUVEN MARTON

Hope Rovelto

Two Sides | 2006

23 X 12 X 12 INCHES (58 X 31 X 31 CM)
Clay
PHOTO BY ARTIST

Graham Campbell

Shoot | 1992

60 X 20 X 38 INCHES (150 X 51 X 95 CM)
Ash, paint
PHOTO BY BOB SCHATZ

This chair is an adaptation and update of a courting chair, stretched out so two people can sit in conversation, finger tip to finger tip at a less intimate distance than with a courting chair. PETER HANDLER

Peter Handler
Conversation Chair | 2004

28 X 72 X 24 INCHES (71 X 180 X 61 CM)
Hardwood frame, aluminum, fabric

PHOTO BY KAREN MAUCH

Alphonse Mattia

Fetish Chair | 2007

35 X 42 X 27 INCHES (88 X 105 X 69 CM)
Russian plywood, various hardwoods, bubinga, vinyl
PHOTOS BY ERIK GOULD

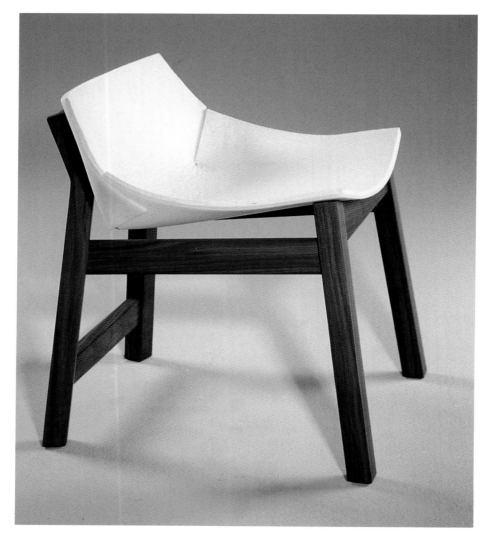

Jennifer Anderson

Drove | 2006

21 X 20 X 20 INCHES (53 X 50 X 50 CM)

Walnut, polyethylene, industrial felt

PHOTO BY LARRY STANLEY

Neil Erasmus
B-Line Chair | 2002

44 X 20 X 22 INCHES (110 X 51 X 56 CM)
Jarrah, pigskin suede
PHOTO BY ROBERT GARVEY

Robert Griffith

Kris Chair | 2006

34 X 24 X 24 INCHES (85 X 61 X 61 CM)
Ash, fabric
PHOTO BY LISA HINKLE

Libby Schrum

Cork Chair | 2006

35 X 19 X 23 INCHES (88 X 48 X 58 CM)

Wood, cork, milk paint

PHOTOS BY JIM DUGAN

Stewart Wurtz

Wenge Chair | 2006

31 X 23 X 22 INCHES (78 X 58 X 56 CM)

Wenge, eucalyptus, fabric

PHOTOS BY ARTIST

Michael Fortune

Untitled | 2005

EACH: 34 X 30 X 28 INCHES (85 X 75 X 70 CM)

Plywood, brass

PHOTO BY MICHAEL CULLEN

John Thoe
Linnea Settee | 2000

35 X 44 X 23 INCHES (88 X 110 X 58 CM)
Cherry
PHOTO BY ARTIST

Larry Buechley
Nancy Buechley
Wishbone Rocker #3 | 2003

41 X 25 X 40 INCHES (103 X 62 X 100 CM)
Cherry, leather
PHOTO BY ADDISON DOTY

Carolyn Grew-Sheridan
"C/Y" Chair | 1994

37 X 19 X 23 INCHES (93 X 48 X 58 CM)
Mahogany
PHOTO BY JOE SCHOPPLEIN

Alexandra Geske

Untitled | 2004

62 X 17 X 22 INCHES (155 X 43 X 56 CM)
Curly maple, leather dye
PHOTO BY ARTIST

J. Michael Floyd

Adirondack 20/20 | 2006

42 X 32 X 44 INCHES (105 X 80 X 110 CM)
Bubinga veneer, painted plywood
PHOTOS BY JOHN LUCAS

Thomas Hucker
Rocker | 2006

37 X 22 X 23 INCHES (93 X 56 X 58 CM)
White oak
PHOTO BY LYNTON GARDNER

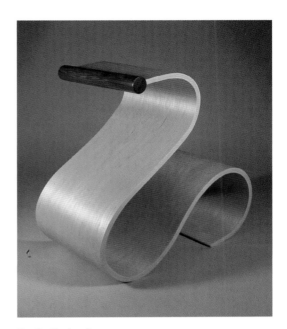

B.G. Pelcak
eVe 6 | 2004

27 X 16 X 28 INCHES (69 X 41 X 71 CM)
Birch plywood, moradillo
PHOTO BY JAY CHIU

Kerry Vesper
Thatza Chair | 2002

34 X 28 X 24 INCHES (85 X 70 X 60 CM)
Bubinga, Baltic birch
PHOTO BY RON DERIEMACKER

Mark Righter
Spring Chair | 2005
30 X 18 X 23 INCHES (75 X 46 X 58 CM)
Reclaimed heart pine, steel spring
PHOTO BY ARTIST

John Morel

Swivel Chair | 1995

42 X 28 X 32 INCHES (105 X 70 X 80 CM)

Redwood ash

PHOTO BY MATTHEW SPIDELL

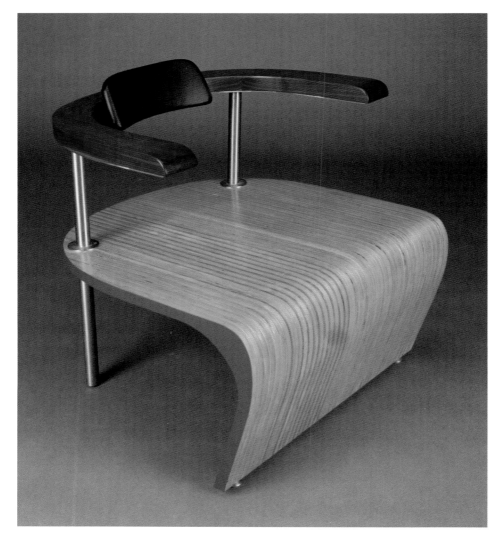

Trevor Wendell

Untitled | 2007

27 X 30 X 25 INCHES (69 X 75 X 64 CM)
Baltic birch, walnut, stainless steel, leather
PHOTO BY CORY ROBINSON

Srdjan Simić

Levat Chair | 2002

30 X 20 X 26 INCHES (75 X 51 X 66 CM)

Cherry, steel

PHOTO BY ARTIST

Sam Maloof
Short Armchair

Sam Maloof
Tall Armchair

Sam Maloof (1916–)

Sam Maloof's chairs have become icons of contemporary furniture. He has won every conceivable award for his work including the American Craft Council's Gold Medal, The Furniture Society's Award of Distinction, and a MacArthur Fellowship. The beautiful form, graceful line, and extreme comfort of his rocking chairs, like the one pictured here, make them the gold standard against which others are measured.

ALL PHOTOS COURTESY OF SAM MALOOF

Sam Maloof
Rocker

Breaking free from a Mennonite heritage, I strived to combine Danish frame and floating plane construction with the freedom and poetics of Maloof(ian)-inspired joinery. How'd I do, Sam?

BILLY STAUFFER

Billy Stauffer

Chair 1 | 2005

37 X 27 X 25 INCHES (93 X 69 X 64 CM)
Oregon black walnut, black leather upholstery

PHOTO BY JOHN STAMETS WITH BILLY STAUFFER

Hank Gilpin

Yewwood Chairs | 1991

EACH: 34 X 22 X 21 INCHES (86 X 56 X 53 CM)

Yewwood, upholstery

PHOTO BY ARTIST
COURTESY OF PRITAM & EAMES GALLERY

Susan Broidy
Body Chair 2 | 2001
37 X 18 X 24 INCHES (93 X 46 X 61 CM)
Plywood
PHOTO BY SCOTT DOOLEY

Howard Werner

Eucalyptus Chair | 1997

33 X 36 X 44 INCHES (83 X 90 X 110 CM)

Eucalyptus

PHOTO BY ARTIST

Richard Bronk

Untitled | 2005

35 X 57 X 24 INCHES (88 X 143 X 60 CM)

Bird's eye maple, Honduran and African mahogany,
wenge, curly maple

PHOTO BY BILL LEMKE

Garry Knox Bennett
New Ladderback | 2004

42 X 15 X 22 INCHES (105 X 38 X 56 CM)
Wood, fabricated ladder

PHOTOS BY M. LEE FATHERREE

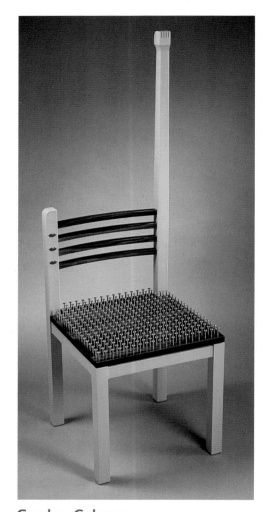

Gordon Galenza

Fakir Goes to Bollywood | 2001

52 X 18 X 18 INCHES (130 X 46 X 46 CM)

Maple, ebony, red jasper, steel rivets, dye, lacquer

PHOTO BY JOHN DEAN PHOTOGRAPHS INC.

Derek Chalfant

Mother's Helper | 2005

96 X 44 X 44 INCHES (240 X 110 X 110 CM)

Dyed curly oak, bronze, aluminum, rubber, steel, powdered milk

PHOTO BY ARTIST

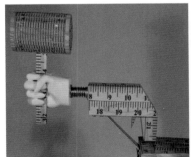

Rob Millard-Mendez

Highchair for a Ruler | 2007

36 X 11 X 14 INCHES (90 X 28 X 36 CM)
Wood, measuring sticks, aluminum
PHOTOS BY ARTIST

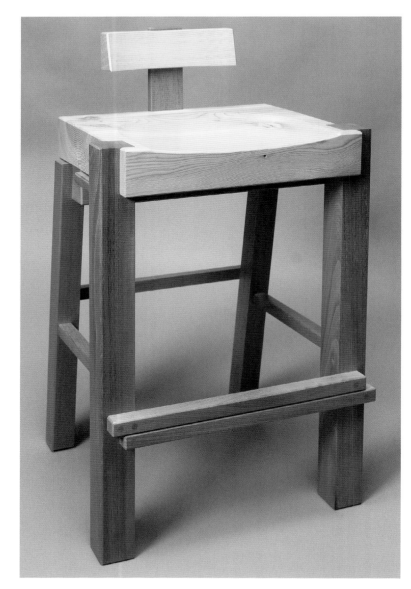

Brad Reed Nelson
Beckerman Bar Stool | 2005
24 X 18 X 19 INCHES (61 X 46 X 48 CM)
Mahogany, reclaimed fir
PHOTO BY CHARLES ABBOTT

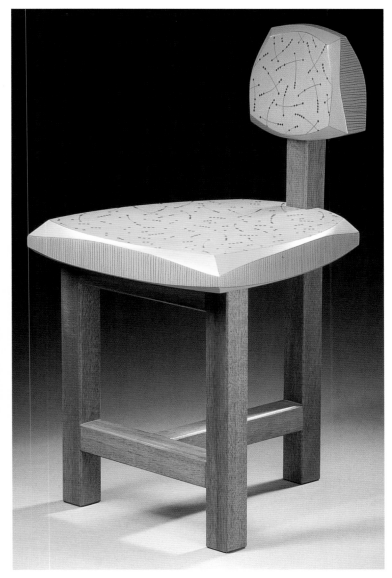

Kimberly Winkle

Children's Yellow Faceted Chair | 2007

26 X 14 X 15 INCHES (66 X 36 X 38 CM)

Mahogany, poplar, graphite

PHOTOS BY JOHN LUCAS

One goal with these chairs is to make a room more sociable. This is accomplished when the two chairs are faced toward each other, making the guest—and not the TV—the focal point. Sean Favero

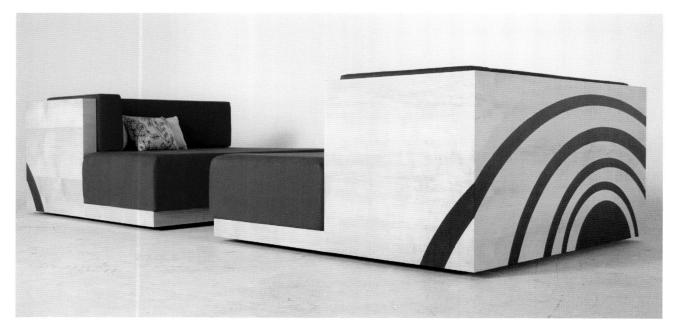

Sean Favero

Big Boy Sofa Chairs | 2007

EACH: 26 X 50 X 50 INCHES (66 X 125 X 125 CM)
Poplar, plywood, maple veneers, foam
PHOTO BY JENICA HEINTZELMAN

Michael Puryear

Barrow Chair | 2003

32 X 29 X 28 INCHES (80 X 73 X 71 CM)
Bubinga, leather
PHOTO BY ARTIST

Todd Ouwehand

Cantilevered Ellipses | 1994

28 X 22 X 24 INCHES (71 X 56 X 61 CM)

Purpleheart, silk upholstery

PHOTO BY MARK ADAMS

Pajda Perina

Chair Marilyn | 2001

43 X 18 X 22 INCHES (108 X 46 X 56 CM)
Jarrah, aluminum, upholstery
PHOTOS BY EDDIE RESERA

Jessica Schlachter-Townsend

OE | 2000

EACH: 36 X 20 X 32 INCHES (90 X 51 X 80 CM)
Acrylic polymer
PHOTO BY JEFFREY CROWELL

Isaac Arms

Steel Chair | 2005

30 X 28 X 45 INCHES (75 X 70 X 113 CM)
Steel, patina, powder coating
PHOTO BY BILL LEMKE

Jack Larimore

Tete à Tete | 2007

40 X 74 X 38 INCHES (100 X 185 X 95 CM)

Paulownia, recycled plastic bottle board, fiberglass, steel

PHOTOS BY ARTIST

Joel Pollock
Victoria | 2007

26 X 72 X 19 INCHES (66 X 180 X 48 CM)
Steel, leather

PHOTO BY BRYNNE KENNEDY

Karen DeLuca

Untitled | 2006

15 X 14 X 32 INCHES (38 X 36 X 80 CM)
Plywood, earplugs, acrylic paint
PHOTOS BY CHARLES DELUCA

Clay Dillard

Tulip Folding Chair | 2001

EACH: 35 X 18 X 9 INCHES (88 X 46 X 23 CM)

Stainless steel, aluminum

PHOTO BY POP GUN PHOTOGRAPHY

This two-seater is not a "loveseat." In this piece, form follows dysfunction. Liz Kerrigan

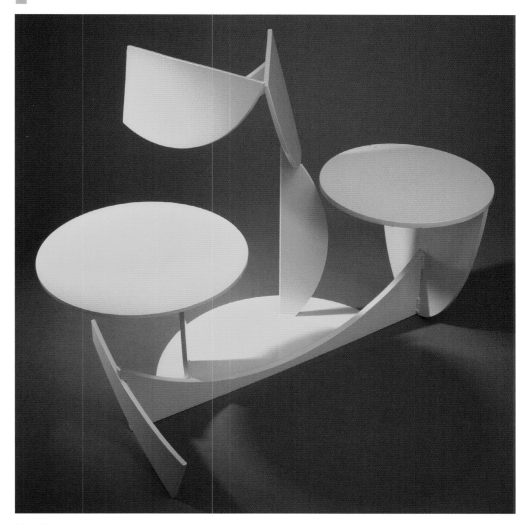

Liz Kerrigan

If You Loved Me, You'd Know | 2000

31 X 42 X 24 INCHES (78 X 105 X 61 CM)
Steel
PHOTO BY JOSEPH SAVANT

Trenton Baylor

Stump | 2005

30 X 24 X 24 INCHES (75 X 61 X 61 CM)
Mahogany, cast bronze
PHOTO BY DON LINTNER

Mark Davis

Flat Steel Chair | 2007

32 X 27 X 22 INCHES (80 X 68 X 55 CM)
Maple veneers, steel, faux leather
PHOTO BY JENICA HEINTZLEMAN

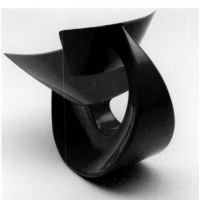

Vivian Beer

Red Rocker | 2007

31 X 21 X 28 INCHES (78 X 53 X 71 CM)

Steel, automotive paint

PHOTOS BY ARTIST

Dean Pulver

Fauna | 2005

35 X 17 X 20 INCHES (88 X 43 X 51 CM)

Walnut, dye, paint

PHOTOS BY PAT POLLARD

Richard H. Sweetman

Tattoo & Ruby's Chair | 2005

EACH: 40 X 19 X 19 INCHES (100 X 48 X 48 CM)
Steel

PHOTO BY ARTIST

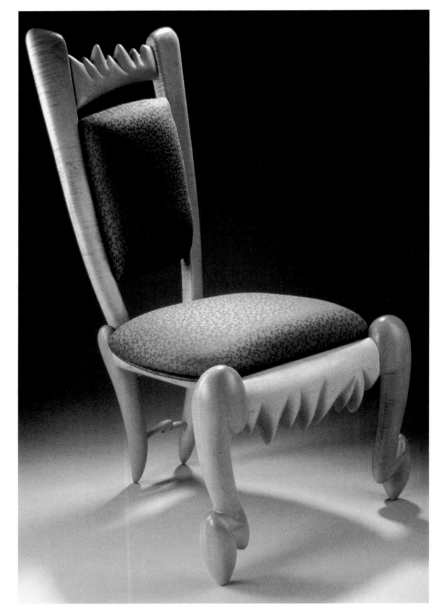

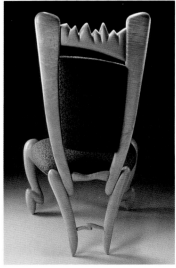

Karen Ernst

Quandary Mountain Dining Chair | 2001

40 X 22 X 24 INCHES (100 X 56 X 61 CM)

Maple, fabric, foam

PHOTOS BY MARK JOHNSTON

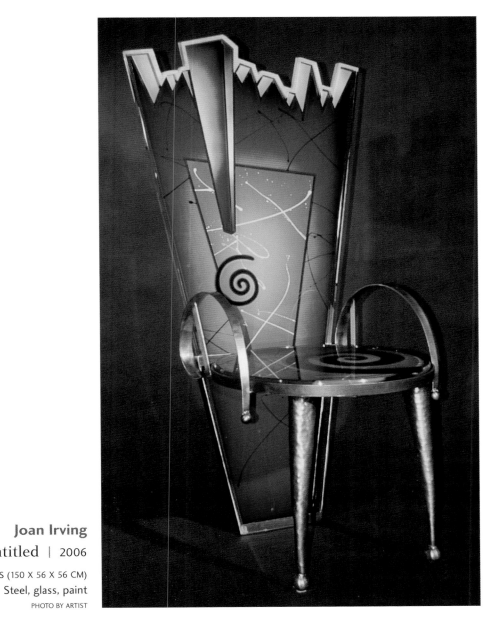

Joan Irving
Untitled | 2006
60 X 22 X 22 INCHES (150 X 56 X 56 CM)
Steel, glass, paint
PHOTO BY ARTIST

Gord Peteran

Ark | 2001

66 X 26 X 48 INCHES (165 X 65 X 120 CM)
Wood, bronze, glass, velvet
PHOTO BY ELAINE BRODIE

Mordechai Schleifer
Couch of Court Peacocks Tail | 2001

34 X 45 X 34 INCHES (85 X 113 X 85 CM)
Toned plywood, velvet
PHOTO BY JONATHAN RACHLINE

Mordechai Schleifer
The Oracles' Arm Chair | 2001

30 X 39 X 31 INCHES (75 X 98 X 78 CM)
Mahogany, aluminum, stainless steel, velvet
PHOTO BY JONATHAN RACHLINE

Rob Hare

Arm Chair | 2007

35 X 38 X 34 INCHES (88 X 95 X 85 CM)
Claro walnut, steel, leather
PHOTOS BY CHRIS KENDALL

Beeken Parsons

Untitled | 2007

35 X 32 X 60 INCHES (89 X 81 X 152 CM)
Curly maple, leather
PHOTO BY ARTIST

Peter Handler

Glider Rocking Chair | 2003

43 X 24 X 28 INCHES (108 X 61 X 71 CM)

Plywood frame, aluminum, fabric

PHOTO BY KAREN MAUCH

James Schriber

Big Chair & Ottoman | 2005

CHAIR: 42 X 30 X 42 INCHES (105 X 75 X 105 CM)

Bubinga, mohair

PHOTO BY JOHN KANE

W. Douglas Allen

Angle Chair | 2005

34 X 39 X 34 INCHES (86 X 98 X 86 CM)
Oak, steel, rubber webbing, foam, batting, velvet
PHOTO BY GWEN AUCOIN

This is the first piece of furniture I designed using cork. I was (and still am) part woodworker, part corksmith. DANIEL MICHALIK

Daniel Michalik

Float | 2003

31 X 26 X 30 INCHES (78 X 66 X 75 CM)
Lacquered beech, cork
PHOTO BY MARK JOHNSTON

Mitch Ryerson
Summer Chair | 2005

40 X 24 X 48 INCHES (100 X 61 X 120 CM)
Marine plywood, copper, aluminum
PHOTOS BY DEAN POWELL

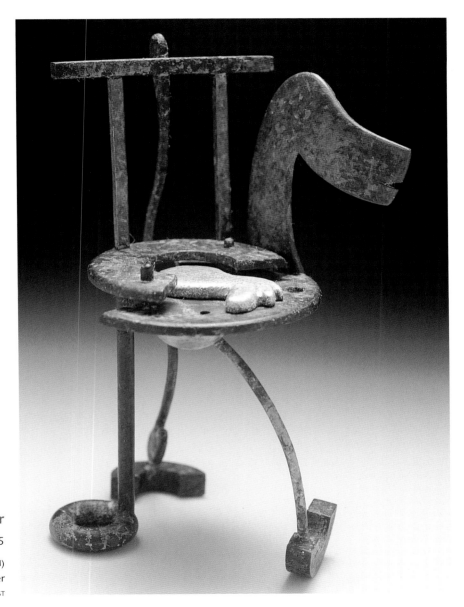

Tom Muir

Chair Transformation | 1995

4 X 3 X 2 INCHES (10 X 8 X 5 CM)

Brass, aluminum, copper

PHOTO BY ARTIST

The surface paint is based on the idea of long-term use, as is seen on public railings that have the layers of paint worn down by years of being touched.

CHRISTOPHER POEHLMANN

Christopher Poehlmann
Scarlet | 2000

34 X 20 X 26 INCHES (85 X 51 X 66 CM)
Steel, auto paint
PHOTOS BY ARTIST

Chris Shea

Café Chairs | 1997

EACH: 36 X 17 X 17 INCHES (90 X 43 X 43 CM)

Steel, glass

PHOTOS BY JOHN LUCAS
COURTESY OF WEXLER GALLERY

Jon Brooks

Matisse | 1999

72 X 27 X 27 (180 X 68 X 68 CM)

Maple, acrylic, color pencil, stain, lacquer, varni

PHOTO BY DEAN POWELL

Kurt R. Schlough
Gazelle Chair | 1994

66 X 21 X 34 INCHES (165 X 53 X 85 CM)
Hard maple, steel, rubber isolators
PHOTO BY ARTIST

Michael Gloor

Window Chair I | 2002

42 X 17 X 16 INCHES (105 X 43 X 41 CM)

Mahogany frame, African satinwood, leather

PHOTO BY DAVID GILSTEIN

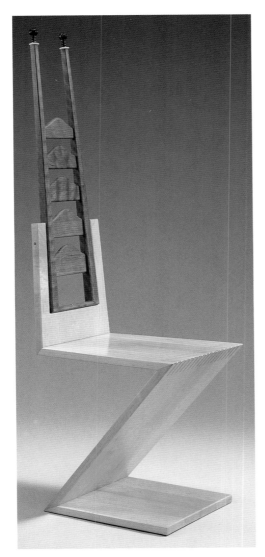

Garry Knox Bennett

Ladderback–Old | 2003

52 X 15 X 17 INCHES (130 X 38 X 43 CM)

Wood, bone, beads, copper

PHOTO BY M. LEE FATHERREE
COURTESY OF LEO KAPLAN MODERN, NY

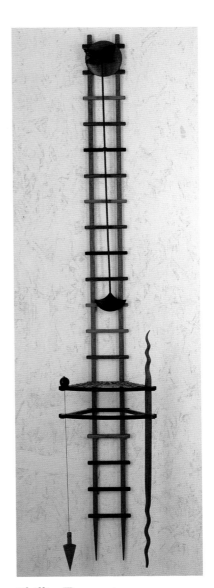

Phillip Tennant

Tick-Tock | 2000

73 X 13 X 10 INCHES (183 X 33 X 25 CM)

Various hardwoods

PHOTO BY PATRICK BENNETT

Anthony Marschak

Spring Chair | 2007

37 X 21 X 17 INCHES (93 X 53 X 43 CM)

Bamboo

PHOTO BY DYLAN MADDUX

Richard Judd

Ribbon Chair | 2003

30 X 20 X 36 INCHES (75 X 51 X 90 CM)
Bubinga, bending ply
PHOTO BY BILL LEMKE

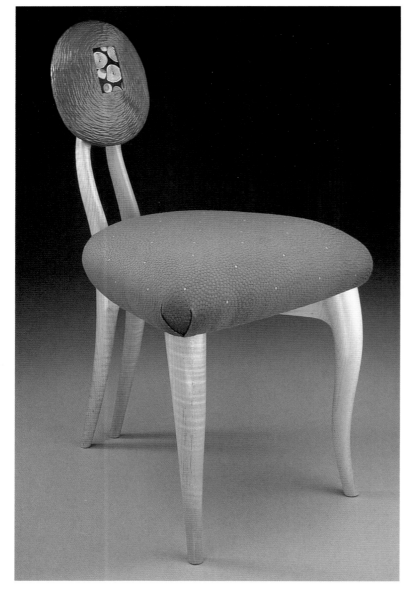

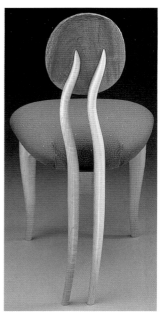

Bonnie Bishoff
J.M. Syron

Phoenix | 2003

20 X 23 X 35 INCHES (51 X 58 X 88 CM)

Mahogany, curly maple, polymer clay, cotton upholstery

PHOTOS BY DEAN POWELL

Aaron Fedarko
Amigo Chair | 2007

40 X 19 X 17 INCHES (100 X 48 X 43 CM)
Cherry, black leather
PHOTO BY JIM DUGAN

Ross Annels
Katerina Chair | 2003–2007

34 X 23 X 22 INCHES (85 X 58 X 56 CM)
Jarrah, upholstery
PHOTO BY ARTIST

Aaron Levine

Konrad Chair | 2005

33 X 18 X 17 INCHES (82 X 46 X43 CM)

European pear, calf leather

PHOTO BY ART GRICE

Catherine Earle

Symbolic Matters | 2006

31 X 31 X 31 INCHES (78 X 78X 78 CM)
Wood, upholstery, textile paint
PHOTO BY MARIE-DOMINIQUE VERDIER

The design process for this chair began with a sampling of animal forms then refined and abstracted into a steel calligrapher's line. This sculpture/chair uses the anthropomorphic history of furniture design as a touchstone and script for imagination. What if chairs gave us tail feathers instead of extra legs and feet? Vivian Beer

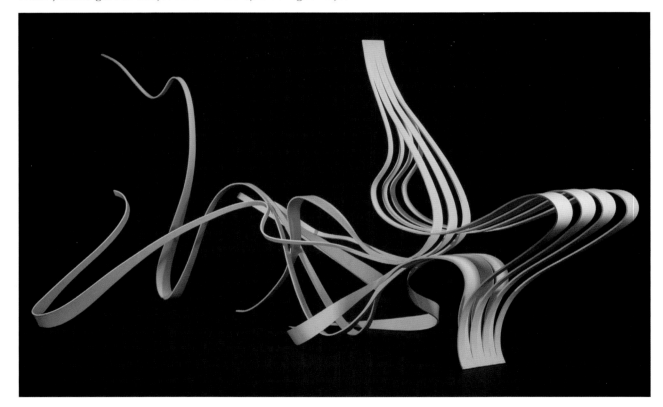

Vivian Beer
Filled with Birds and Beasts | 2004

92 X 54 X 36 INCHES (230 X 135 X 90 CM)
Steel, enamel paint
PHOTO BY JAY YORK

John Makepeace
Trine | 1998

32 X 23 X 21 INCHES (80 X 58 X 53 CM)
Yew wood, bog oak
PHOTO BY ARTIST

Taeyoul Ryu

Black Cat | 1998

72 X 18 X 47 INCHES (180 X 46 X 118 CM)
Poplar, plywood, aluminum, leather
PHOTOS BY SYLVIA L. ROSEN

Christopher Poehlmann

Red Rocker | 2001

40 X 24 X 48 INCHES (100 X 61 X 120 CM)

Aluminum, paint

PHOTO BY ED CHAPPELL

This chair is stable for entering, exiting, and tasking, yet rocks for relaxation. The extended front leg discourages overzealous rocking by the childlike. PETER DANKO

Peter Danko
Equilibrium | 2005

33 X 23 X 27 INCHES (84 X 58 X 69 CM)
Ply-bent beech, seat-belt material
PHOTO BY ANDY FRANCK

Garry Knox Bennett

Sylvia's Chair | 2004

31 X 22 X 25 INCHES (78 X 56 X 64 CM)

Wood, rattan, paint

PHOTO BY M. LEE FATHERREE

Janice C. Smith

Whimcycle | 1995

31 X 53 X 27 INCHES (78 X 133 X 68 CM)

Plywood, steel tubing, rubber wheels, upholstery

PHOTO BY REUBEN WADE

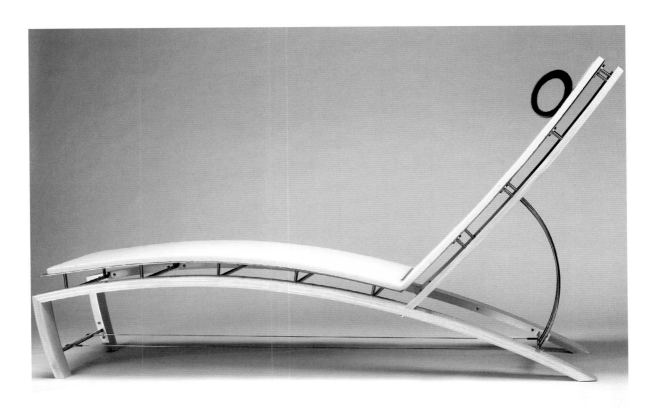

Richard Prisco
Bare Naked Chaise | 2004

36 X 22 X 72 INCHES (90 X 55 X 180 CM)
Sycamore, aluminum, stainless steel, felt
PHOTOS BY JOSEPH BYRD

Paul Piacitelli
Side Chair | 2007

26 X 26 X 26 INCHES (65 X 65 X 65 CM)
Maple-apple plywood
PHOTO BY TOM COLLICOTT

David Colwell
C3 Stacking Chair | 1991

EACH: 34 X 21 X 21 INCHES (85 X 53 X 53 CM)
Ash
PHOTO BY ARTIST

Robert Hendrickson
Untitled | 2006

31 X 25 X 27 INCHES (78 X 64 X 69 CM)
Ash, cherry
PHOTO BY JOE SCHOPPLEIN

Michael Gilmartin

The Gilmartin Chair | 2002

33 X 26 X 37 INCHES (83 X 66 X 93 CM)

Marine fir plywood, black walnut

PHOTO BY CHARLES AKERS PHOTOGRAPHY

Howard Werner

Eucalyptus Chair | 1997

46 X 45 X 48 INCHES (115 X 113 X 120 CM)

Eucalyptus

PHOTO BY ARTIST

Gregg Lipton

Cherry Rocker | 1990

42 X 24 X 42 INCHES (107 X 61 X 107 CM)
Cherry
PHOTO BY STRETCH TUEMMLER

John Morel

Cherry Rocking Chair | 2006

40 X 26 X 30 INCHES (100 X 66 X 75 CM)

Cherry, bird's eye maple

PHOTO BY MATTHEW SPIDELL

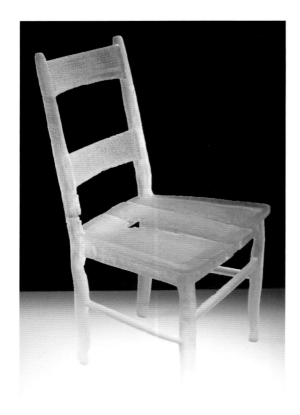

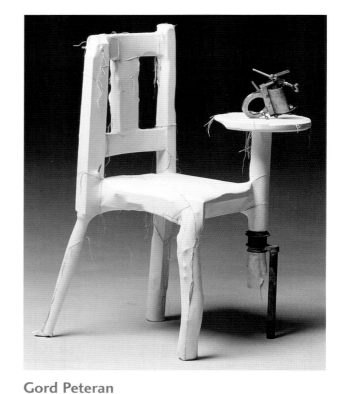

Peter Fleming
Burnt Chair | 2006

32 X 18 X 17 INCHES (80 X 46 X 43 CM)
Cast urethane
PHOTO BY ARTIST

Gord Peteran
Study Station | 2006

28 X 14 X 17 INCHES (70 X 36 X 43 CM)
Wood, leather, brass
PHOTO BY ELAINE BRODIE

Roger Hauge
Rosemarie Hohol
Reflection | 2003

44 X 28 X 23 INCHES (110 X 71 X 58 CM)
Peeled and dyed maple, hand-woven cotton
PHOTO BY ROGER HAUGE

Brian Boggs
Untitled | 2006

41 X 19 X 19 INCHES (103 X 48 X 48 CM)
Ebonized white oak, iron, woven hickory bark
PHOTOS BY LOUIS CAHILL

Tim Hintz

Blue and White Settin' Chair | 2005

36 X 16 X 19 INCHES (90 X 40 X 48 CM)
Wood, hickory bark, milk paint
PHOTO BY JOHN LUCAS

Harriete Estel Berman

Material Identity | 2001

38 X 17 X 14 INCHES (95 X 43 X 36 CM)
Recycled tin cans, aluminum, sterling silver, gold rivets, steel screws

PHOTOS BY PHILIP COHEN

Suzan Germond

Swirl Chair | 2000

34 X 17 X 16 INCHES (85 X 43 X 40 CM)

Antique wood chair, vitreous glass tile, ceramic tile, broken china, flat back marbles

PHOTOS BY CAL RICE

The back of the chairs are incise carved with Morse code and my intuitive signature hieroglyphics. The Morse code reads "Relax, have a seat." MARK DEL GUIDICE

Mark Del Guidice
Sanfra Chairs | 2006

EACH: 38 X 17 X 20 INCHES (95 X 43 X 51 CM)
Curly maple, milk paint, upholstery, lacquer
PHOTO BY CLEMENTS/HOWCROFT

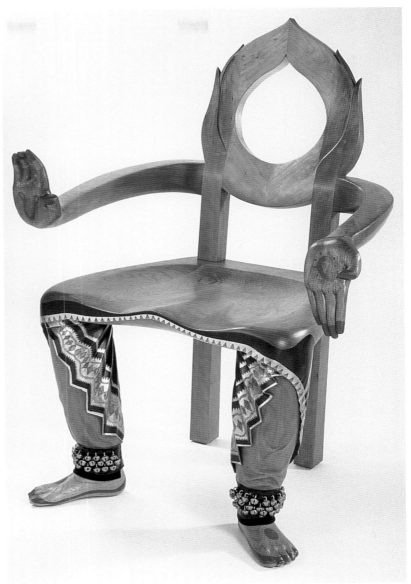

Sabiha Mujtaba
Bharatanatyam Dancer | 2004

41 X 27 X 24 INCHES (103 X 68 X 62 CM)
Cherry, polychrome, transfer gold leaf, bells
PHOTOS BY BART KASTEN

Dale Lewis
Nude Negotiating the Stares | 2004

68 X 25 X 23 INCHES (170 X 63 X 58 CM)
Dyed maple, natural pink ivory, velour upholstery
PHOTO BY ARTIST

Sylvie Rosenthal
Untitled | 2004

51 X 23 X 26 INCHES (128 X 59 X 66 CM)
Steel, upholstery
PHOTO BY WALKER MONTGOMERY

Jon Brooks

True Loves Blue | 2000

52 X 52 X 28 INCHES (130 X 130 X 70 CM)

Maple, acrylic, color pencil, stain, lacquer, varnish

PHOTO BY DEAN POWELL
COURTESY OF CURRIER MUSEUM OF ART

Paul Reiber

Sun's Hands | 1992

61 X 24 X 18 INCHES (153 X 64 X 46 CM)
Cherry, walnut, gold leaf, fabric
PHOTO BY JESS SHIRLEY

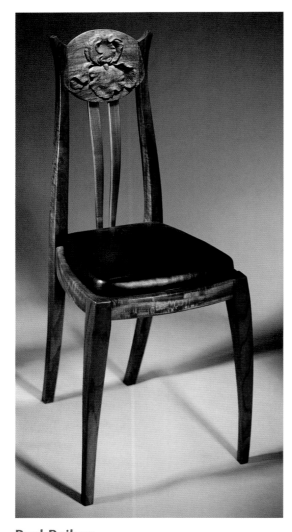

Paul Reiber

Small Iris Chair | 1999

38 X 16 X 16 INCHES (95 X 41 X 41 CM)
Claro walnut, leather
PHOTO BY MARK SAFFRON

Paul Reiber

Love Seat | 2000

35 X 31 X 18 INCHES (88 X 78 X 46 CM)
Walnut, leather
PHOTO BY MARK SAFFRON

Garry Knox Bennett

Chair | 2005

34 X 28 X 32 INCHES (85 X 71 X 80 CM)

Wood, copper with matt-silver plate, upholstery, paint

PHOTO BY M. LEE FATHERREE
COURTESY OF LEO KAPLAN MODERN, NY

Douglas Finkel

Source Bench | 1999

16 X 27 X 12 INCHES (41 X 69 X 31 CM)

Poplar, paint, rope

PHOTO BY DOUBLE IMAGE STUDIOS
COLLECTION OF THE RENWICK GALLERY, SMITHSONIAN INSTITUTION

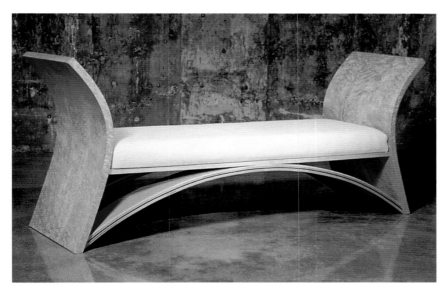

Andrew Muggleton
Lotus Bench | 2003

31 X 71 X 23 INCHES (78 X 178 X 58 CM)
Bird's eye maple veneer, wenge, ultrasuede
PHOTO BY ARTIST

Robert Spangler
Doig Bench | 2000

26 X 60 X 16 INCHES (66 X 150 X 40 CM)
Oregon walnut
PHOTO BY MARK VAN S.

Katherine Ortega

Shoe Valet | 2001

72 X 17 X 62 INCHES (180 X 43 X 155 CM)
Mahogany, cedar, maple, plywood,
pewter knobs and pulls, velvet
PHOTO BY JIM WILDEMAN

Cameron Van Dyke

Dr. Starr | 2005

36 X 46 X 33 INCHES (90 X 115 X 83 CM)

Steel, leather

PHOTO BY SHIPPERT

Jack Larimore

Natural Desire | 2003

EACH: 54 X 24 X 24 INCHES (135 X 60 X 60 CM)

Paulownia, ash, bronze, felt

PHOTOS BY JOHN CARLANO

Jack Larimore

Abide | 2007

32 X 44 X 34 INCHES (80 X 110 X 85 CM)
Paulownia, steel, epoxy resin
PHOTO BY ARTIST

Sam Batchelor

Untitled | 2004

36 X 62 X 24 INCHES (90 X 155 X 60 CM)

Bubinga, steel

PHOTOS BY ARTIST

Benjamin Harth

Untitled | 2006

34 X 20 X 22 INCHES (85 X 51 X 56 CM)

Plywood, cherry veneer

PHOTO BY THEODOR S. RZAD

Samuel Provenza
Paperclip Chair | 2006

26 X 20 X 25 INCHES (65 X 51 X 64 CM)
Stainless steel, anigre veneer, walnut veneer
PHOTO BY ARTIST

Tobias Feltus
Chair2 | 2003

EACH: 29 X 16 X 19 INCHES (73 X 41 X 48 CM)
Birch, steel, urethane rubber finish
PHOTO BY ARTIST

Peter Danko

EcoEden 2 | 1981

EACH: 33 X 21 X 22 INCHES (84 X 53 X 55 CM)

Beech

PHOTO BY DAVID SHARPE
COLLECTION OF MUSEUM OF MODERN ART, NY

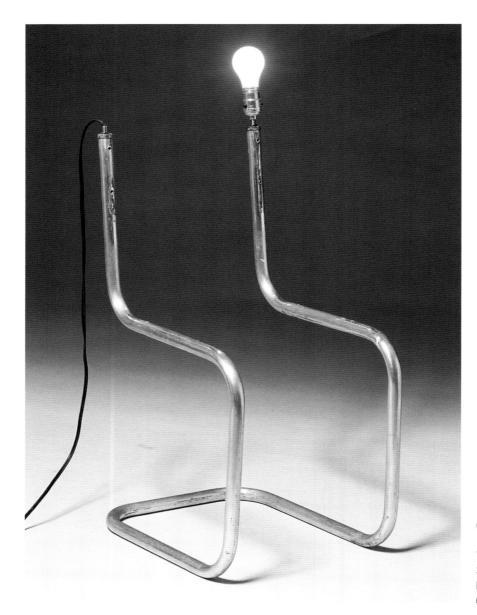

Gord Peteran
Electric Chair | 2005

27 X 15 X 20 INCHES (69 X 38 X 51 CM)
Found metal frame, electricity
PHOTO BY ELAINE BRODIE

Adam Jones
128 lbs. | 2007
36 X 18 X 23 INCHES (90 X 46 X 58 CM)
Poplar, steel, automotive paint
PHOTOS BY CHRISTINA ELTON

Curtis K. LaFollette

1216/01 | 2001

35 X 26 X 30 INCHES (88 X 65 X 75 CM)

Stainless steel, aluminum

PHOTO BY NASH STUDIO

David Colwell

C10 Springback Chair | 2005

38 X 20 X 20 INCHES (95 X 50 X 50 CM)

Ash, stainless steel

PHOTO BY ARTIST

Paul M. Minniti

SuperDan | 2001

14 X 26 X 90 INCHES (36 X 48 X 225 CM)
Anodized aluminum, stainless steel, vinyl
PHOTOS BY ARTIST

Brad Reed Nelson

The Cult of Charles and Ray | 1999

24 X 24 X 34 INCHES (61 X 61 X 85 CM)

Cherry, steel, aluminum, rollerblade wheels, wool

PHOTO BY ALAN MCCOY

Brad Reed Nelson

The Execuglide Chair | 2000

35 X 24 X 36 INCHES (88 X 61 X 90 CM)

Chechen wood, steel

PHOTO BY ALAN MCCOY

215

This piece is made up of interlocking repeatable units that allow the chair to be adjusted and reconfigured into other designs. GREGORY LAVOIE

Gregory Lavoie

Arthropod | 2007

31 X 18 X 36 INCHES (78 X 46 X 90 CM)

Baltic birch, plywood

PHOTOS BY ARTIST

Jordan Gehman

Low Rider | 2007

30 X 16 X 46 INCHES (75 X 41 X 115 CM)

Maple, bleached maple

PHOTO BY LARRY STANLEY

Jacob Knudsen

Rocking Goat | 2006

35 X 30 X 33 INCHES (88 X 75 X 83 CM)
Maple, stainless steel, goat hide, foam
PHOTO BY ARTIST

Mike Farruggia

Plywood Rocker | 2000

32 X 25 X 36 INCHES (80 X 64 X 90 CM)
Plywood, threaded rod, cap nuts
PHOTO BY ARTIST

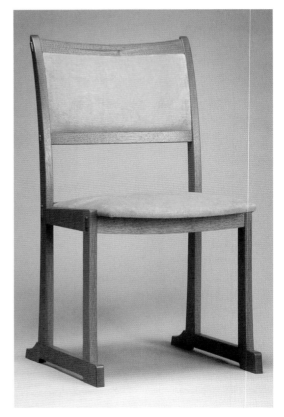

Luke Peart

High Back Chair | 2005

60 X 18 X 32 INCHES (150 X 46 X 80 CM)
Cherry, upholstery, aluminum pins
PHOTO BY ARTIST

Ejler Hjorth-Westh

Dogma | 2006

36 X 18 X 18 INCHES (90 X 46 X 46 CM)
Kwila, velvet
PHOTO BY KEVIN SHEA

A sea urchin from the Philippines provided the inspiration for this chair. On its shell, the uneven ordering of the attachment points for the spines provides a strong pattern. Ross Annels

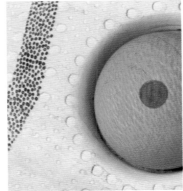

Ross Annels

Echinoid Chair | 2004

72 X 20 X 21 INCHES (180 X 51 X 53 CM)

Silver ash, jarrah, silky oak

PHOTO BY GEOFF POTTER; DETAIL BY ANDREA HIGGINS

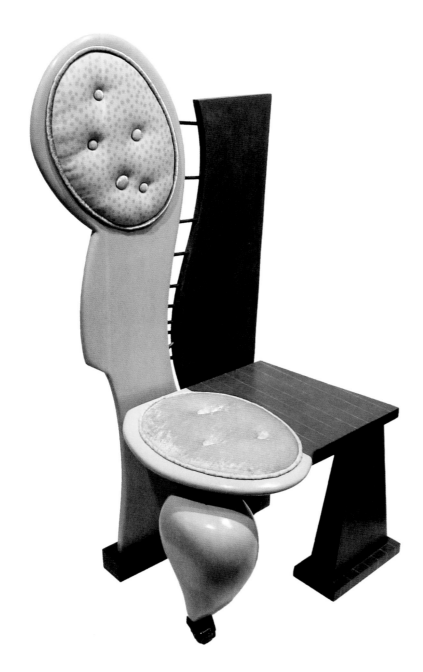

Steven T. Samson
Me, Myself and I | 2004

53 X 25 X 20 INCHES (133 X 64 X 51 CM)
Mahogany, basswood, milk paint, acrylic, brass, found object, fabric

PHOTO BY JEFFREY L. MEEYWSEN
COURTESY OF KENDALL COLLEGE OF ART AND DESIGN

Garry Knox Bennett

Duncan Rietveld | 2003

40 X 15X 18 INCHES (100 X 38 X 46 CM)
Dyed mahogany, lacewood, gold-plated brass

PHOTO BY M. LEE FATHERREE
COURTESY OF LEO KAPLAN MODERN, NY

Gordon Galenza

Uhuru Chair | 1999

52 X 18 X 18 (130 X 46 X 46 CM)

Jatoba, bloodwood, ebony, pau amarelo, malachite

PHOTO BY JOHN DEAN PHOTOGRAPHS INC.

Robert Erickson

2 Tashjian Chairs | 1997

EACH: 48 X 24 X 24 INCHES (120 61 X 61 CM)
Maple, bubinga, leather

PHOTO BY ARTIST

Heather Allen-Swarttouw
Leisure Chair

Harriete Estel Berman
UPC Consuming Identity

Each of the miniature chairs on these two pages was created and donated by a well-established craft artist for Chairity, an annual collection of miniatures used by the Craft Emergency Relief Fund (CERF) to raise funds for and increase awareness of its work assisting artists who have had career-threatening emergencies. The Chairity collection encompasses a wide variety of media and techniques. Each chair is designed to fit within a 4-inch (10.2 cm) cube. Information about CERF can be found at www.craftemergency.org.

Merrill Morrison
Checkered Chair

Aaron Kramer
Beyond the Tipping Point

Hope Rovelto
Twin High Chairs

Jo Stone
Untitled

ALL PHOTOS BY GLENN MOODY

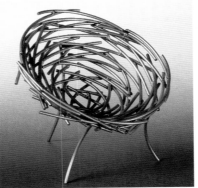

Julie Girardini
Nest Chair

Dale Broholm
Untitled

Susan kavicky
Mandatory Leisure

Jennifer Violette
Blue Comfy Chair

Dean Pulver
Fauna

Jerilyn Virden
Untitled

Michael Gilmartin
Avos Armchair | 1994

34 X 26 X 34 INCHES (85 X 53 X 85 INCHES)
Marine fir plywood, black walnut

PHOTOS BY CHARLEY AKERS PHOTOGRAPHY

Heath Matysek-Snyder
Stealth Chair | 2002

40 X 18 X 22 INCHES (100 X 46 X 56 CM)
Maple, steel, plywood
PHOTO BY BILL LEMPKE

Michael Gloor

Fan Chair 2 | 2007

EACH: 40 X 16 X 16 INCHES (100 X 41 X 41 CM)

Cherry, ebony inlays, leather

PHOTO BY DAVID GILSTEIN

My inspiration for this chair comes from the Notre Dame Cathedral in Paris. I enjoy creating furniture that evolves from architecture with strong visual appearance.

DENNIS P. SCHLENTZ

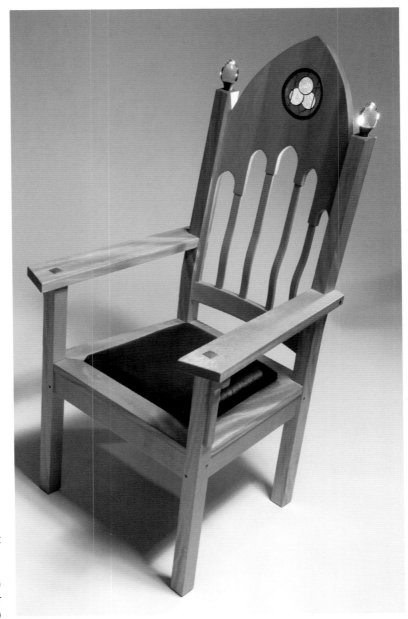

Dennis P. Schlentz
Queen's Chair | 2001

50 X 24 X 23 INCHES (125 X 61 X 58 CM)
Pau amarelo wood, stained glass, leather
PHOTO BY JOHN LAWS (JL IMAGING)

231

Chris Martin

1400 R24 Club Chair | 2001

31 X 37 X 31 INCHES (78 X 93 X 78 CM)

Wood, steel, rubber

PHOTO BY GEORGE ENSLEY

Paul Lynch
Arches | 2005

40 X 18 X 21 INCHES (100 X 46 X 53 CM)
Wood, rubber, cotton
PHOTOS BY ARTIST

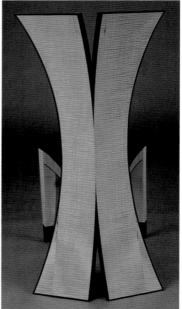

Todd Graves

Untitled | 2007

35 X 17 X 18 INCHES (88 X 43 X 46 CM)

Curly maple, wenge, leather

PHOTOS BY ARTIST

Leah Woods

Cape-Back Chair | 2007

32 X 19 X 24 INCHES (80 X 48 X 61 CM)
Walnut, Australian walnut veneer, sheepskin, black dye, brass
PHOTOS BY JAMES SCHUYLER

Kyle P. Zimmerman

Ava | 2007

38 X 17 X 17 INCHES (97 X 43 X 43 CM)
Ribbon mahogany, African blackwood, calf leather
PHOTOS BY HELM STUDIOS

Lynn Szymanski
A Chair for Sending and Receiving | 2007

48 X 24 X 21 INCHES (120 X 61 X 53 CM)
Poplar, milk paint, vinyl, linen
PHOTOS BY UNH PHOTO SERVICES

Brindan Byrne
Joan Irving
Seats Du Verre Glass Chairs | 2000

EACH: 60 X 24 X 22 INCHES (150 X 61 X 56 CM)
Ebonized wood, glass, leather

PHOTO BY KEN WEST

James Schriber

Untitled | 2005

EACH: 30 X 20 X 18 INCHES (75 X 51 X 46 CM)

Dyed curly maple

PHOTO BY JOHN KANE

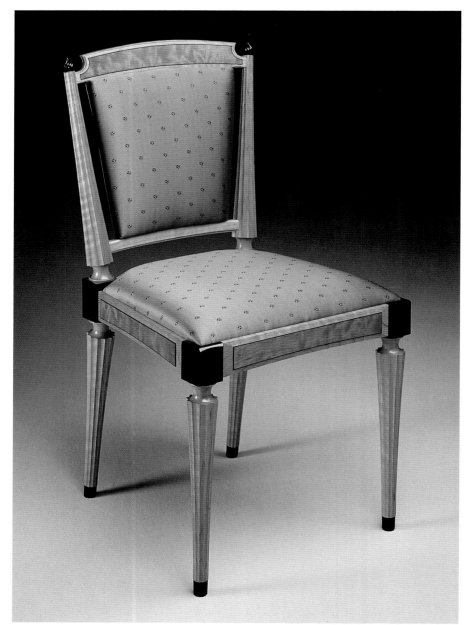

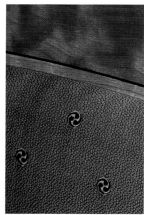

Richard Scott Newman
Cherry Fluted Chair | 1997

35 X 18 X 19 INCHES (88 X 46 X 48 CM)
Cherry, ebony, silk
PHOTOS BY DAVID J. LEVEILLE

Alf Sharp

Biedermeier Redux | 1998

34 X 26 X 21 INCHES (85 X 66 X 53 CM)

Sycamore, andiroba, paint

PHOTO BY TONY MAUPIN

Kristina Madsen
Chairs | 1990

EACH: 38 X 19 X 18 INCHES (95 X 48 X 46 CM)

Maple, silk

PHOTO BY ARTIST

Kristina Madsen

Tea Couch | 2006

38 X 85 X 28 INCHES (95 X 213 X 70 CM)
Bubinga, dyed pearwood, ebony, linen
PHOTO BY DAVID STANSBURY

Robert Griffith

Hemma Chair | 2006

32 X 24 X 22 INCHES (80 X 61 X 56 CM)
Ash, fabric
PHOTO BY LISA HINKLE

Peter Dellert

Haystack Chair | 2000–2005

EACH: 37 X 18 X 20 INCHES (93 X 46 X 51 CM)
Curly maple, maple veneer, walnut,
cotton upholstery
PHOTO BY JOHN POLAK

Michael Grace

Dining Chairs | 2004

EACH: 33 X 18 X 18 INCHES (83 X 46 X 46 CM)
Black cherry, Karelian birch
PHOTO BY ARTIST

John Rodie
Atomic Chair | 2007
31 X 18 X 16 INCHES (78 X 45 X 40 CM)
Cherry
PHOTO BY ARTIST

Yusuke Hoshii
Untitled | 2007

31 X 16 X 17 INCHES (78 X 41 X 43 CM)
Japanese oak
PHOTO BY ARTIST

Yvonne Mouser

Transmogrificates | 2005

ALL: 31 X 68 X 36 INCHES (78 X 170 X 90 CM)

Douglas fir

PHOTO BY WILFRED J. JONES

The bookmatched wood grain runs lengthwise along the seat and converges at the center, adding to the joined and mirrored conversation. YVONNE MOUSER

Yvonne Mouser
Conjoined | 2004

33 X 44 X 44 INCHES
Elm
PHOTO BY WILFRED J. JONES

Kenton Hall

Straddle Chairs | 1987

EACH: 31 X 17 X 17 INCHES (78 X 43 X 43 CM)

Maple, oak, pine, milk paint

PHOTO BY DEAN POWELL

Michael Fortune

Untitled | 2006

EACH: 32 X 22 X 20 (80 X 56 X 51 CM)

Cherry

PHOTO BY ARTIST

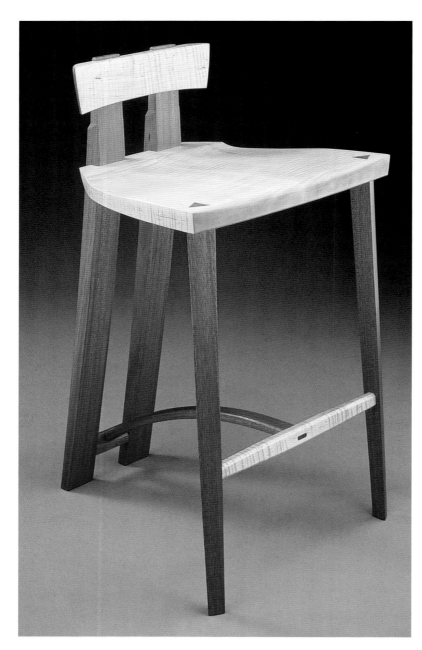

Timothy Rousseau
Kitchen Chair | 2003

31 X 18 X 18 INCHES (79 X 46 X 46 CM)
Curly maple, mahogany
PHOTO BY DEAN POWELL

John Clark

Moon Chair | 2001

EACH: 42 X 18 X 19 INCHES (107 X 46 X 48 CM)

Mahogany, quilted maple, ebony

PHOTO BY TIM BARNWELL

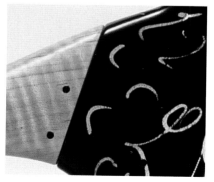

Jon Brooks

Styx Ladderback | 1996

EACH: 84 X 24 X 24 INCHES (210 X 60 X 60 CM)
Maple, acrylic, lacquer, varnish
PHOTOS BY FRANK CORDELL

Jacque Allen
Mockintosh Ladder Back Chair | 2005

58 X 20 X 20 INCHES (145 X 50 X 50 CM)
Cherry, African blackwood, birch, buffalo hide
PHOTOS BY ARTIST

Lepo

Untitled | 2005

59 X 26 X 24 INCHES (148 X 66 X 61 CM)

Pickled maple, cherry, cocobolo,
ebonized basswood

PHOTOS BY MICHAEL AYERS

Scott Braun

b&w | 2003

42 X 22 X 20 INCHES (105 X 56 X 50 CM)
Ebonized mahogany, calfskin
PHOTO BY ERIC MCNATT

Christine Lee
Black Line Chair | 2000

40 X 24 X 26 INCHES (100 X 61 X 66 CM)
Wood, acrylic
PHOTO BY ARTIST

Garry Knox Bennett
Rietveld Redux Chair | 2004

33 X 24 X 21 INCHES (84 X 61 X 54 CM)
Wood, beads, paint
PHOTO BY M. LEE FATHERREE

M. Hosaluk
Tower of Chair | 2006
174 X 30 X 30 INCHES (435 X 75 X 75 CM)
Wood, acrylic paint
PHOTO BY ARTIST

Tor Faegre

Oak & Buckthorn Chair | 2000

36 X 30 X 24 INCHES (90 X 75 X 61 CM)
Oak, buckthorn
PHOTO BY ARTIST

M. Hosaluk
In Oakland | 2006

CHAIR: 30 X 18 X 18 (75 X 46 X 46 CM)
Wood, mixed media
PHOTOS BY ARTIST

Carol Townsend

Southwest Stools | 2001

EACH: 10 X 11 X 11 INCHES (25 X 28 X 28 CM)
Clay
PHOTO BY K.C. KRATT

Ted Vogel

Campfire Stories—Stump Stool | 2005

28 X 22 X 22 INCHES (71 X 56 X 56 CM)

Clay

PHOTOS BY BILL BACHHUBER

James Schriber

Untitled | 2002

EACH: 36 X 20 X 20 INCHES (90 X 51 X 51 CM)

Walnut, Macassar ebony

PHOTO BY JOHN KANE

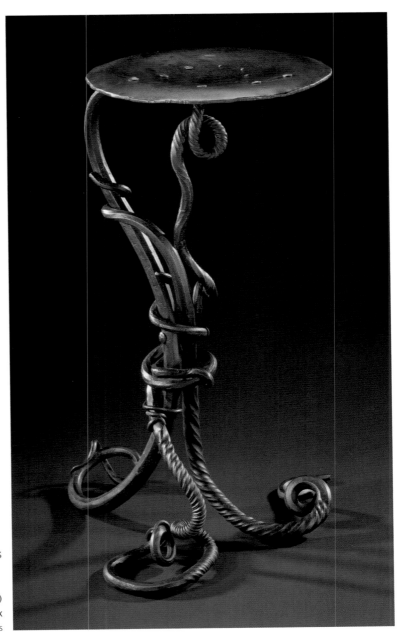

George Rousis

Root Down | 2001

30 X 13 X 20 INCHES (75 X 33 X 51 CM)
Iron, brass, wax
PHOTO BY CHRIS DENNIS

Patty Nelson

Oak Leaf Chair | 2003

84 X 17 X 19 INCHES (213 X 43 X 48 CM)

Copper, steel

PHOTOS BY JOE SCHOPPLEIN

Mirtha Aertker
Doll Chair—Story Tallers | 2007

24 X 5 X 7 INCHES (61 X 13 X 18 CM)
Steel
PHOTO BY ARTIST

Mirtha Aertker
Doll Chair—Story Tellers | 2007

32 X 16 X 3 INCHES (80 X 41 X 8 CM)
Steel
PHOTO BY ARTIST

This miniature chair disassembles into earrings of gold, silver, and iolite; a reversible pendant; an etched pin that forms the seat; and a box (the seat) that holds a two-part chain with finials that match the earrings.

NOËL YOVOVICH

Noël Yovovich
More Than Meets the Eye | 2001

4 X 2 X 3 INCHES (10 X 5 X 8 CM)
Sterling silver, titanium, gold, iolites
PHOTOS BY LARRY SANDERS

Paul Freundt

Swept Back Chair | 1994

36 X 30 X 25 INCHES (90 X 75 X 64 CM)

Stainless steel

PHOTO BY BRYAN MOREHEAD

Vivian Beer

Spine | 2005

34 X 25 X 27 INCHES (85 X 63 X 68 CM)
Stainless steel
PHOTO BY ARTIST

Po Shun Leong

Left/Center/Right Chair | 2007

35 X 47 X 25 INCHES (88 X 118 X 64 CM)

Rock maple, polypropylene

PHOTO BY ARTIST
COURTESY OF PRIMAVERA GALLERY, CA

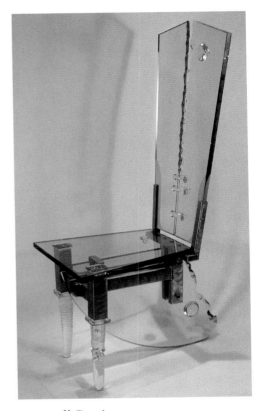

Maxwell Davis

Untitled | 2004

50 X 18 X 26 INCHES (125 X 46 X 66 CM)

Stainless steel, glass

PHOTO BY ARTIST

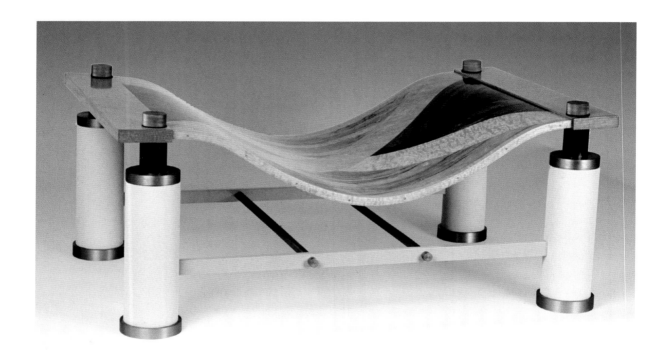

Romeu-Richard Furniture

Veneered Ottoman | 2004

17 X 30 X 20 INCHES (43 X 75 X 51 CM)

Aluminum, veneered laminate, fabric, paint

PHOTO BY ARTIST
COURTESY OF WEXLER GALLERY, PA

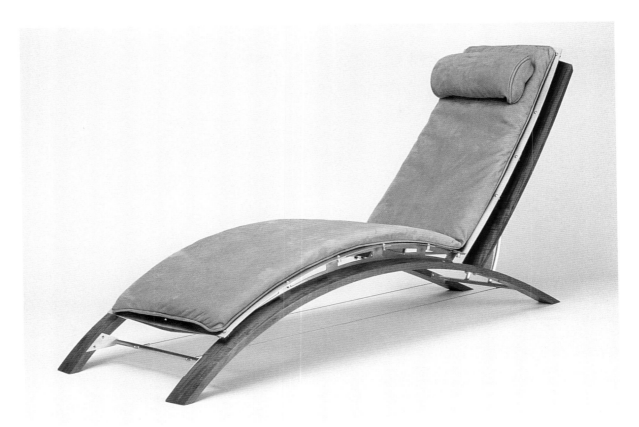

Richard Prisco
Chaise #2 | 1997–2004

36 X 22 X 78 INCHES (90 X 55 X 195 CM)
Mahogany, aluminum, stainless steel, leather
PHOTOS BY PAUL NURNBERG

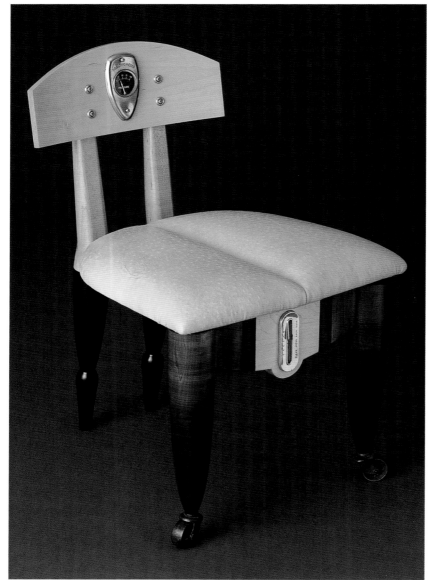

Kim Kelzer

Lap Dance Chair | 2004

30 X 23 X 18 INCHES (75 X 58 X 46 CM)
Maple, leather, found objects, fake fur
PHOTOS BY RACHEL OLSSEN

Gord Peteran

Two | 2006

18 X 64 X 14 INCHES (46 X 160 X 36 CM)

Walnut, brass

PHOTO BY ELAINE BRODIE

Lee A. Schuette
Wood Chip Chair | 2005

16 X 20 X 17 INCHES (41 X 51 X 43 CM)
Vinyl, wood chips
PHOTO BY ARTIST

Ladislav Czernek

B+ Chair | 2003

33 X 17 X 22 INCHES (83 X 43 X 56 CM)

Redwood burl veneer, plywood, foam core

PHOTO BY RICK MENDOZA

Chad Aldridge

Flame On! | 2005

50 X 30 X 34 INCHES (125 X 75 X 85 CM)

Cherry, patina

PHOTOS BY ARTIST

Liz Kerrigan
After You (No. 2) | 2007
40 X 12 X 16 INCHES (100 X 31 X 41 CM)
Steel, galvanized nails
PHOTO BY JOSEPH SAVANT

Dean Wilson

Untitled | 2003

34 X 20 X 26 INCHES (86 X 51 X 66 CM)

Fiberglass, foam, painted steel

PHOTOS BY ARTIST

Joel Green

Living Lounge | 2006

30 X 96 X 38 INCHES (75 X 240 X 95 CM)
Poplar, fiberglass, microsuede
PHOTO BY MARK JOHNSTON

Graham Campbell

Cone Chair | 1995

24 X 20 X 24 INCHES (61 X 51 X 61 CM)
Ash, walnut veneer, bent plywood, paint
PHOTO BY JOHN LUCAS

Dean Pulver

My Friend | 2004

32 X 27X 26 INCHES (80 X 68 X 65 CM)
Dyed walnut
PHOTO BY PAT POLLARD

Paul Freundt

Naxos | 2000

28 X 18 X 22 INCHES (70 X 46 X 56 CM)

Steel, patina

PHOTO BY BRYAN MOREHEAD

David W. Scott

Low Back Ripple Stool | 2007

34 X 20 X 20 INCHES (85 X 51 X 51 CM)

Maple, milk paint

PHOTO BY TIM BARNWELL

Andy Buck

Moon Beam | 2001

34 X 18 X 20 INCHES (85 X 46 X 51 CM)
Wood, paint
PHOTO BY BILL BACHHUBER

Gregg Lipton
Untitled | 1991

EACH: 36 X 18 X 18 INCHES (91 X 46 X 46 CM)
Bleached ash
PHOTO BY STRETCH TUEMMLER

Wendy Maruyama
Mickey Macintosh | 1982
60 X 30 X 16 INCHES (150 X 75 X 41 CM)
Poplar, paint
PHOTO BY MICHAEL JAMES SCATTERY

Tom Loeser
Ladderbackkcabreddal | 2005

EACH: 87 X 41 X 21 INCHES (218 X 103 X 53 CM)
Wood, paint
PHOTO BY BILL LEMKE

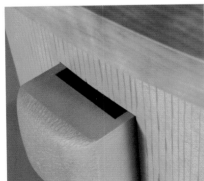

Chris Bowman

Chair with Drawers | 2006

41 X 18 X 17 INCHES (103 X 46 X 43 CM)

Cherry, birch veneer plywood, milk paint

PHOTOS BY ARTIST
COURTESY OF TERCERA GALLERY, CA

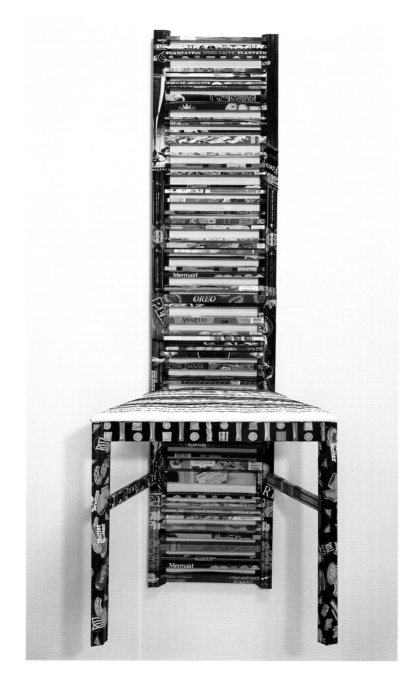

Harriete Estel Berman

Consuming Identity | 2001

51 X 20 X 10 INCHES (128 X 50 X 26 CM)

Recycled tin cans, steel, screws, aluminum and sterling silver rivets, fabric

PHOTO BY PHILIP COHEN

Marie Kline
Curved Chair #1 | 2007

48 X 24 X 22 INCHES (120 X 61 X 56 CM)
Maple, bending plywood, cottonwood, walnut
PHOTOS BY FRANK MARQUEZ

Craig Nutt

Celery Chair with Peppers, Carrots & Snow Peas | 2005

37 X 25 X 22 INCHES (93 X 63 X 55 CM)

Wood, leather, lacquer

PHOTOS BY DEBORAH WIYGUL

Christopher Poehlmann

Chunky Chair | 2004

32 X 24 X 20 INCHES (80 X 61 X 51 CM)

Aluminum, paint

PHOTO BY ED CHAPPELL

M. Hosaluk

Cactus Chair | 2006

38 X 20 X 20 INCHES (95 X 51 X 51 CM)

Wood, acrylic paint

PHOTO BY ARTIST

Mitch Ryerson

Harp Chairs | 2003

EACH: 16 X 17 X 20 INCHES (41 X 43 X 51 CM)
Baltic birch, maple, paint
PHOTO BY DEAN POWELL

Andy Buck

Blossfeldt Chairs | 1996

EACH: 27 X 36 X 25 INCHES (69 X 90 X 64 CM)

Wood, upholstery, paint

PHOTO BY DEAN POWELL

Craig Nutt

Burning | 2002

46 X 57 X 31 INCHES (115 X 143 X 78 CM)
Wood, paint, handwoven fabric by Janet Taylor
PHOTO BY JOHN LUCAS

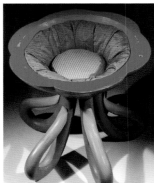

Ann Walsh

Otamotafloria Sitdownicus | 2005

24 X 14 X 14 INCHES (61 X 36 X 36 CM)

Basswood, upholstery

PHOTOS BY ANTHONY PEREZ

The *"miniachair"* series began as original acrylic paintings by Carolyn Schmitz depicting imaginary chairs composed entirely of desert plant material. Imagine yourself as the miniature inhabitant of the desert in order to experience the chairs as full size.

LARRY FAGAN AND CAROLYN SCHMITZ

Larry Fagan
Carolyn Schmitz

Hi-Back Agave Chair | 2005

10 X 5 X 4 INCHES (25 X 13 X 10 CM)
Polymer clay, acrylic paint, desert plant materials
PHOTOS BY LARRY FAGAN
COURTESY OF VAN GOGH'S EAR GALLERY, AZ

Larry Fagan
Carolyn Schmitz

Patio Chair | 2005

6 X 4 X 4 INCHES (15 X 10 X 10 CM)
Wood-based modeling clay, acrylic paint, desert plant
materials
PHOTO BY LARRY FAGAN
COURTESY OF VAN GOGH'S EAR GALLERY, AZ

Larry Fagan
Carolyn Schmitz

Striped Lounge | 2005

6 X 12 X 6 INCHES (15 X 31 X 15 CM)
Polymer clay, acrylic paint, desert plant materials
PHOTO BY LARRY FAGAN
COURTESY OF VAN GOGH'S EAR GALLERY, AZ

Rob Hare

Dining Chairs | 1996

EACH: 36 X 18 X 21 INCHES (90 X 46 X 53 CM)
Cherry, mahogany, steel
PHOTO BY RALPH GABRINER

My initial inspiration came from rebuilding an original Rietveld "Z" chair. I played with angles and curves until the chair became comfortable and the design my own.

ROB HARE

Wesley A. Crosby
Spindel 1 and Spindel 2 | 1998

EACH: 36 X 23 X 35 INCHES (90 X 58 X 88 CM)
Binding plywood, cast aluminum
PHOTO BY STAR KOTOWSKI

Wesley A. Crosby

Stool | 1998

31 X 13 X 19 INCHES (78 X 33 X 48 CM)
Padauk, stainless steel
PHOTOS BY ARTIST

Adrienne M. Grafton

Disconnected | 2004

EACH: 4 X 2 X 2 INCHES (10 X 5 X 5 CM)

Copper, silver

PHOTO BY ROBERT DIAMANTE

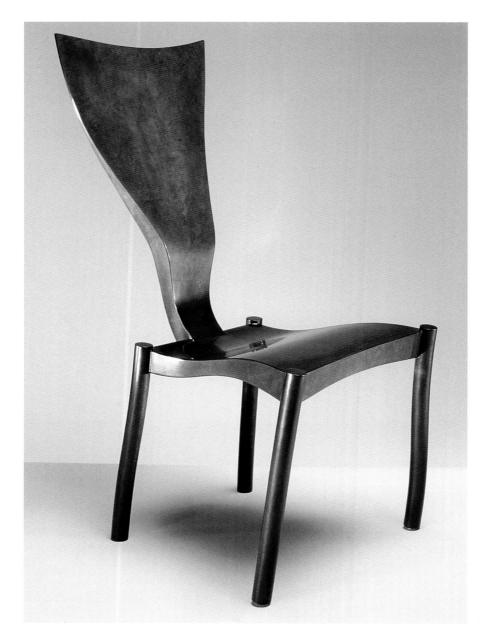

Paul Freundt

Poseidon | 1996

44 X 21 X 24 INCHES (110 X 54 X 61 CM)
Steel, patina
PHOTO BY BRYAN MOREHEAD

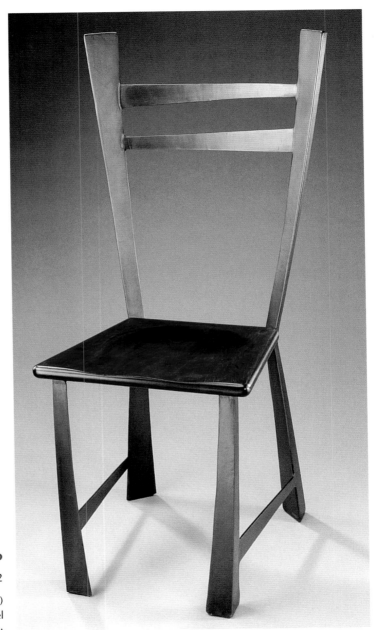

Chajo

Bowed Game Chair | 2002

44 X 16 X 16 INCHES (110 X 41 X 41 CM)

Maple, steel

PHOTO BY HAP SAKWA

*The chair here is taken apart;
new legs, back, and posts are
fabricated/carved; and then it is
aged appropriately. Ease is always
an illusion.* EDWARD HENDERSON

Edward Henderson
Untitled | 2001

80 X 13 X 15 INCHES (200 X 33 X 38 CM)
Wood, canvas, oil paint
PHOTOS BY GARY GRAVES

Michael J. Saari

Deconstruction Chair | 1997

36 X 24 X 18 INCHES (90 X 60 X 45 CM)
Iron, polychrome paint
PHOTO BY VIRGE LORENTZ

Alexis Moran

Lookout | 2004

84 X 30 X 48 INCHES (213 X 76 X 122 CM)
Steel
PHOTO BY BRIAN MORAN

Hope Rovelto
Metal Chair | 2005

23 X 12 X 12 INCHES (58 X 31 X 31 CM)
Clay
PHOTO BY ARTIST

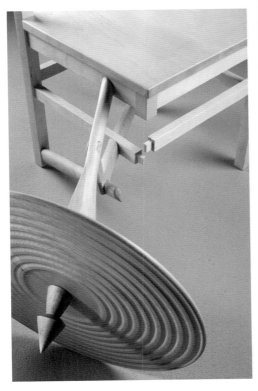

Jordan Gehman

Rollin' on 20" | 2007

30 X 33 X 29 INCHES (75 X 83 X 73 CM)
Maple, bleached maple
PHOTOS BY LARRY STANLEY

Tom Loeser
*Chair*³ | 2003

VARIABLE DIMENSIONS
Maple, mahogany, paint
PHOTO BY ARTIST

Lee A. Schuette
Untitled | 2005

39 X 20 X 19 INCHES (98 X 51 X 48 CM)
Curly maple, aluminum, tennis racquet string
PHOTO BY DOUG PRINCE

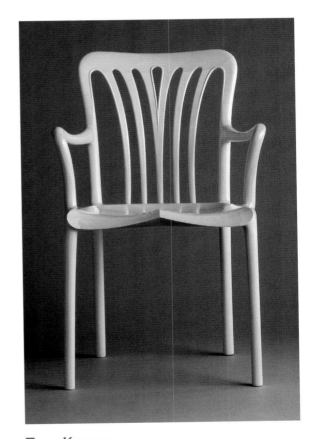

Tony Kenway
Huon Armchair | 2004

35 X 18 X 19 INCHES (88 X 45 X 48 CM)
Tasmanian huon
PHOTO BY DAVID YOUNG

Yusuke Hoshii

Untitled | 2004–2005

EACH: 19 X 14 X 14 INCHES (48 X 36 X 36 CM)

Yellow poplar, plywood

PHOTO BY HIROZO SANO

Garry Knox Bennett
Upholstered Chair | 2001

35 X 21 X 24 INCHES (88 X 53 X 61 CM)
Steel, plastic ties
PHOTO BY M. LEE FATHERREE

Richard Bubnowski

Diana Chair | 2006

EACH: 27 X 33 X 33 INCHES (68 X 82 X 82 CM)

American cherry, ebony, holly

PHOTO BY PAUL S. BARTHOLOMEW

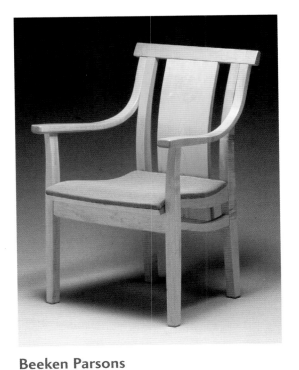

Beeken Parsons
Untitled | 2004

35 X 25 X 21 INCHES (89 X 64 X 53 CM)
Maple, linen
PHOTO BY ARTIST

Nicola D'Agnone
Untitled | 2007

30 X 33 X 26 INCHES (75 X 83 X 66 CM)
White oak, foam, upholstery, lacquer
PHOTO BY ARTIST

Ply-bending uses wood for chairs roughly nine times more efficiently than solid wood. Peter Danko

Peter Danko

Opera Verde | 1998

EACH: 37 X 18 X 23 INCHES (94 X 46 X 58 CM)
Beech
PHOTO BY ANDY FRANCK

Jennifer Anderson

Material Series | 2006

EACH: 29 X 15 X 16 INCHES (73 X 38 X 41 CM)

Mud, wax, ash

PHOTOS BY LARRY STANLEY

Erik Salisbury
Untitled | 2004

45 X 21 X 40 INCHES (113 X 53 X 100 CM)
Eastern maple, steel
PHOTOS BY ARTIST

Jonny Doan

1:1 | 2006

30 X 23 X 22 INCHES (75 X 58 X 56 CM)

Maple-apple plywood, aluminum spacers, threaded rod, hexcap screws

PHOTO BY ARTIST

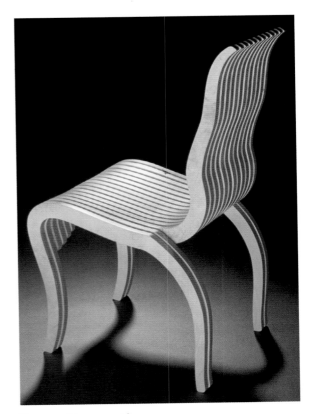

Danny Kamerath

Susan | 1991

36 X 17 X 22 INCHES (90 X 43 X 56 CM)

Baltic birch plywood

PHOTO BY KENT KIRKLEY

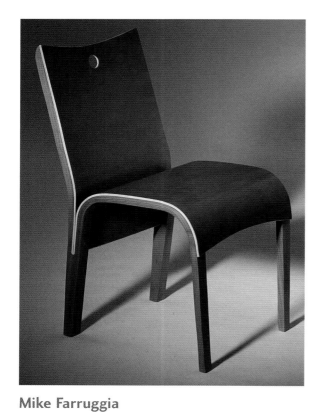

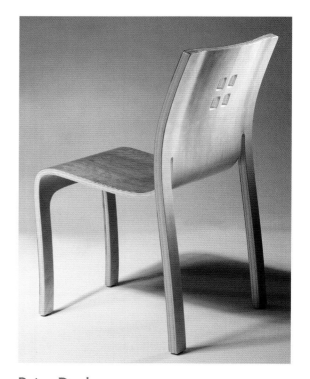

Mike Farruggia

Allegra Chair | 2000

30 X 16 X 20 INCHES (75 X 41 X 51 CM)

Ash, plywood, milk paint

PHOTO BY ARTIST

Peter Danko

EcoEden 1 | 1981

33 X 21 X 22 INCHES (84 X 53 X 55 CM)

Beech

PHOTO BY MARK BOURSHELT
COLLECTION OF MUSEUM OF MODERN ART, NY

W. Douglas Allen

Kleine Curve Chair | 2004

24 X 27 X 30 INCHES (60 X 68 X 75 CM)

Mahogany, oak, industrial casters,
foam, upholstery,

PHOTOS BY GWEN AUCOIN

Peter Handler

Caruso Chair | 2006

39 X 33 X 30 INCHES (98 X 83 X 75 CM)
Hardwood frame, aluminum, fabric

PHOTO BY KAREN MAUCH

W. Douglas Allen

Curve Chair II | 2006

EACH: 25 X 26 X 31 INCHES (63 X 65 X 78 CM)

Mahogany, plywood, rubber webbing, foam, batting, faux
suede upholstery

PHOTO BY ARTIST

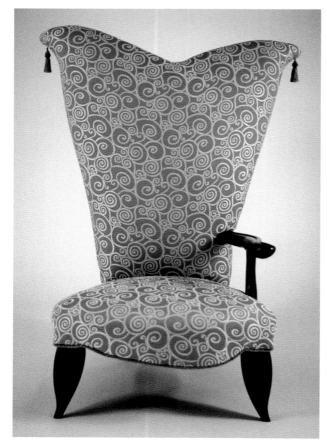

Katherine Ortega
Slipper Chair | 1999

49 X 26 X 37 INCHES (123 X 65 X 93 CM)
Poplar, painted maple, upholstery
PHOTO BY ARTIST

This chair was made by placing a canvas drop cloth over a rocking chair. After resin was applied to the canvas, the rocking chair was removed, leaving a fully functional chair. ANN WALSH

Ann Walsh
Untitled *(For Thalia)* | 2006

48 X 36 X 36 INCHES (120 X 90 X 90 CM)
Polyester resin, canvas
PHOTO BY ARTIST

Neil Stewart

Wing Back Bean Bag | 2007

26 X 31 X 37 INCHES (66 X 78 X 93 CM)

Bean bag pellets, upholstery

PHOTO BY ARTIST

Bonnie Bishoff
J.M. Syron
Star Chair | 2002

30 X 23 X 30 INCHES (75 X 58 X 75 CM)
Cherry, polymer clay veneer, faux leather
PHOTOS BY DEAN POWELL

Janice C. Smith

Lateen | 1995

38 X 66 X 24 INCHES (95 X 165 X 61 CM)

Plywood, torsion box, composite veneer

PHOTO BY REUBEN WADE

Neil Erasmus

Kama Seatra | 1997

31 X 16 X 62 INCHES (78 X 41 X 155 CM)

Oak veneer, paulownia, stainless steel

PHOTOS BY ROBERT GARVEY

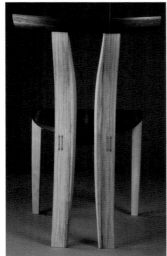

Timothy Rousseau
Austerity Chair | 2004

33 X 18 X 22 INCHES (84 X 46 X 55 CM)
Ash, walnut
PHOTOS BY JIM DUGAN

Robert Erickson

Connemara Chair | 2007

45 X 23 X 26 INCHES (113 X 58 X 66 CM)
Ebonized elm, bubinga
PHOTO BY ARTIST

Michael Fortune

Untitled | 2002

EACH: 34 X 24 X 26 INCHES (85 X 61 X 66 CM)
Macassar ebony, silver, mother pearl
PHOTO BY MICHAEL CULLEN

Stewart Wurtz

Luna Rocker | 2004

35 x 24 x 31 inches (88 x 61 x 78 cm)

Ebonized walnut, steel, fabric

PHOTOS BY ARTIST

Mark Koons

A Simple Chair #1 | 2005

32 X 26 X 20 INCHES (80 X 66 X 51 CM)
Beech, kangaroo leather, milk paint
PHOTO BY K.C. KEEFER

Susan Dunkerley

Vanishing Point | 2004

54 X 9 X 10 INCHES (135 X 23 X 25 CM)
Steel, sandblasted stained glass, silver gelatin
emulsion, graphite
PHOTO BY ARTIST

Emily Greene

Bøje Chair | 2005

32 X 20 X 44 INCHES (80 X 51 X 110 CM)

Steel, woven natural cane

PHOTO BY WILLIAM GREENE

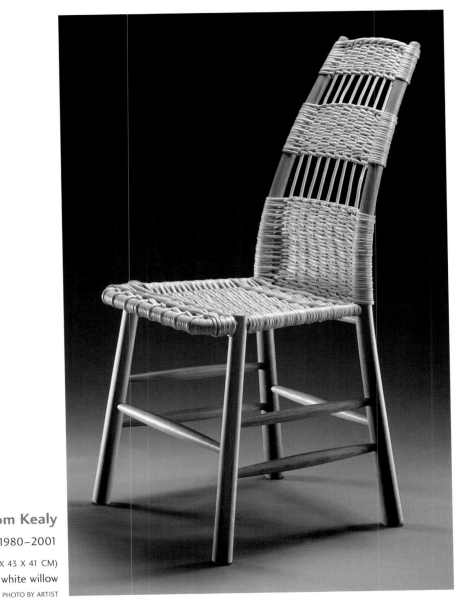

Tom Kealy

Somerset Chair | 1980–2001

42 X 17 X 16 INCHES (105 X 43 X 41 CM)

Ash, woven white willow

PHOTO BY ARTIST

Robert Howard

Untitled | 1998

40 X 25 X 25 INCHES (100 X 64 X 64 CM)
Eucalyptus
PHOTO BY JAMES LATTER

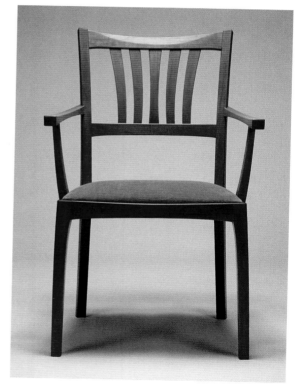

Ejler Hjorth-Westh

Elsinore Armchair | 2002

36 X 22 X 22 INCHES (90 X 50 X 50 CM)
Swiss pear, velvet
PHOTO BY KEVIN SHEA

Brian Newell

Armchair | 2004

34 X 26 X 20 INCHES (86 X 66 X 51 CM)

Materials unknown

PHOTO BY YOSHIAKI KATO
COURTESY OF PRITAM & EAMES GALLERY, NY

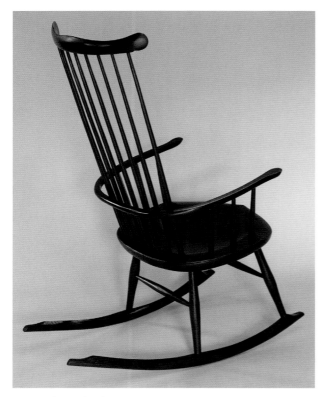

Curtis Buchanan
Sack-Back Armchair | 1988

38 X 25 X 20 INCHES (97 X 64 X 51 CM)
Maple, oak, pine, milk paint
PHOTO BY TOM PARDUE

Timothy Clark
Waltham Rocker | 2006

45 X 24 X 34 INCHES (124 X 61 X 86 CM)
Ash, poplar, cherry, basswood, milk paint
PHOTO BY ARTIST

Cameron Van Dyke

Little Josh | 2005

35 X 32 X 30 INCHES (88 X 80 X 75 CM)

Welded steel

PHOTO BY SHIPPERT

Jonathan Delp

Rejection of Tradition | 2006

30 X 25 X 30 INCHES (75 X 64 X 75 CM)
Mahogany, canary wood, upholstery
PHOTO BY ARTIST

Jacob Cress

Self-Portrait | 2003

40 X 20 X 18 INCHES (100 X 50 X 46 CM)

Walnut, cherry

PHOTO BY BOB VAUGHAN

Alf Sharp

Philadelphia Armchair | 1991

38 X 27 X 21 INCHES (95 X 69 X 53 CM)

Walnut

PHOTO BY TONY MAUPIN

Heath Matysek-Snyder

Slat Chair #1 | 2002

29 X 19 X 18 INCHES (73 X 48 X 36 CM)

Maple, nails

PHOTO BY BILL LEMPKE
COURTESY OF SPRUCE CREEK GALLERY, VA

Danny Kamerath

Sandra | 2006

30 X 17 X 20 INCHES (75 X 43 X 51 CM)

Jatoba wood

PHOTO BY JOSEPH SAVANT

Ania Wagner
Untitled | 2006

EACH: 15 X 15 X 20 INCHES (38 X 38 X 51 CM)
Mahogany
PHOTO BY ARTIST

Takanobu Sekito
Untitled | 2007

DIMENSIONS UNKNOWN
Walnut, plywood, curly maple veneer
PHOTO BY PHIL TENNANT

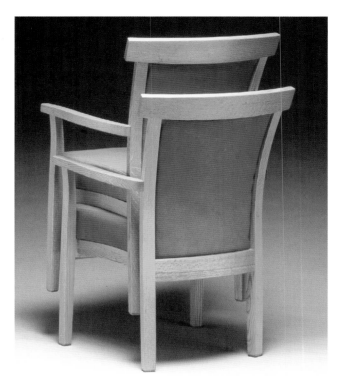

Beeken Parsons

St. Mikes, Stacked | 2003

EACH: 37 X 24 X 24 INCHES (94 X 61 X 61 CM)
Red oak, leather
PHOTO BY ARTIST

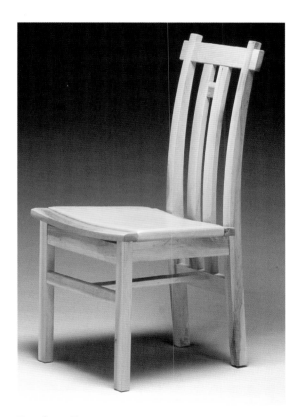

Beeken Parsons
Untitled | 2006

39 X 20 X 20 INCHES (99 X 51 X 51 CM)
Hop hornbeam, leather
PHOTO BY ARTIST

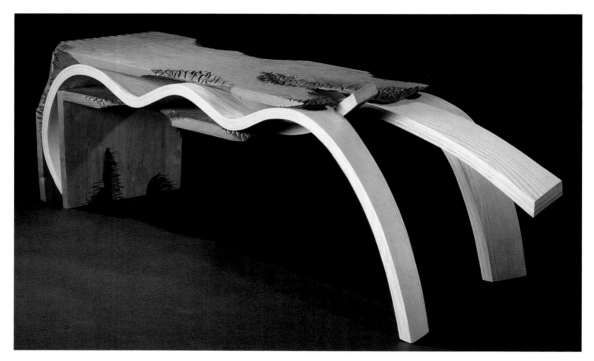

Seth A. Barrett

Corrugated Bench | 1999

17 X 63 X 21 INCHES (43 X 158 X 53 CM)

Ash, Spanish cedar, oil pigments

PHOTO BY FRANK IANOTTI

> *I enjoy both working with and subverting the expectations that a seat should be recognizable, physically comfortable, and appear structurally sound.* MICHAEL OLESON

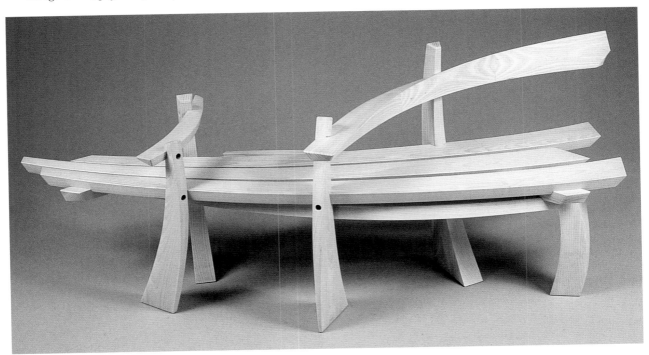

Michael Oleson

Fence Bench | 2004

33 X 80 X 24 INCHES (83 X 200 X 61 CM)

Bleached ash

PHOTOS BY ARTIST

John McDermott

Kechu Chair | 2000

41 X 20 X 18 INCHES (103 X 51 X 46 CM)
Cherry, leather
PHOTO BY MARTIN FOX

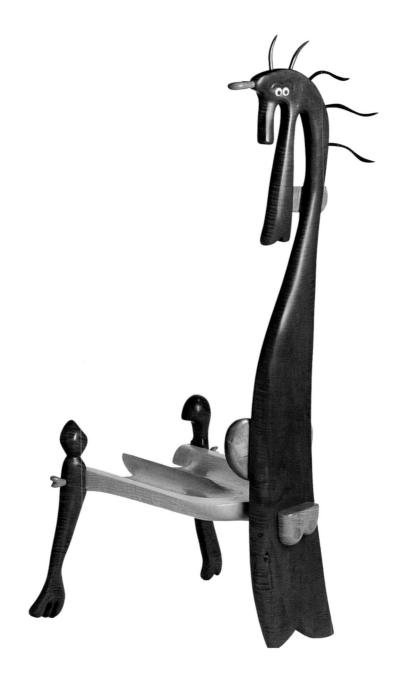

Dale Lewis

Gastropodafemme | 2005

70 X 29 X 31 INCHES (175 X 73 X 78 CM)

Dyed and natural ash, maple, cherry, rosewood, holly, ebony

PHOTO BY RALPH ANDERSON

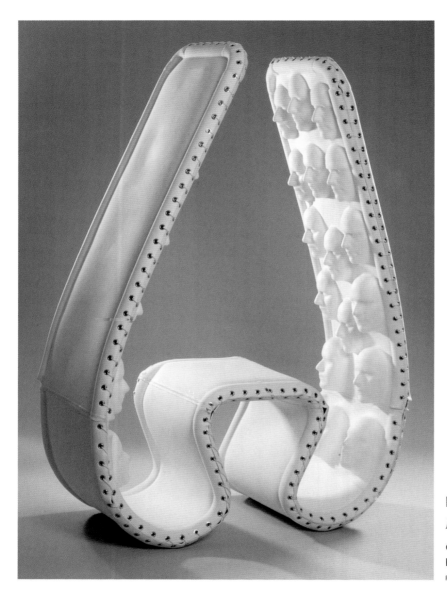

Nava Silberberg

Me, Myself and I | 2005

67 X 47 X 20 INCHES (170 X 120 X 50 CM)

Iron

PHOTO BY ODED ANTMAN

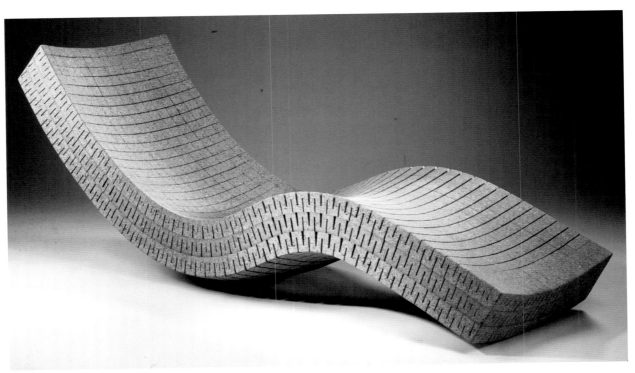

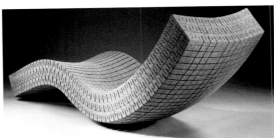

Daniel Michalik

Cortiça | 2004

26 X 20 X 72 INCHES (66 X 51 X 180 CM)

Cork

PHOTOS BY MARK JOHNSTON

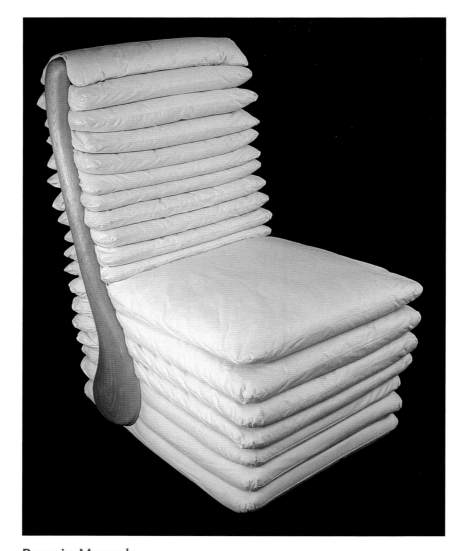

Rosario Mercado

Pillow Chair | 1996

38 X 23 X 27 INCHES (95 X 58 X 69 CM)

Wood, down, cotton

PHOTO BY ARTIST

Garry Knox Bennett

Great Granny Rietveld | 2003

31 X 15 X 18 INCHES (78 X 38 X 46 CM)

Wood, upholstery

PHOTO BY M. LEE FATHERREE
COURTESY OF LEO KAPLAN MODERN, NY

Yekaterina Lutsker

Tango Chair | 2005

31 X 46 X 29 INCHES (78 X 115 X 73 CM)
Purpleheart, yellowheart
PHOTO BY ARTIST

John McDermott

Easel Chair | 1987

30 X 22 X 22 INCHES (75 X 56 X 56 CM)
Oak
PHOTO BY MARTIN FOX

Carolyn Grew-Sheridan

Reader's Chair | 1996

47 X 45 X 35 INCHES (118 X 113 X 88 CM)

Maple, maple plywood, paint

PHOTO BY JOE SCHOPPLEIN

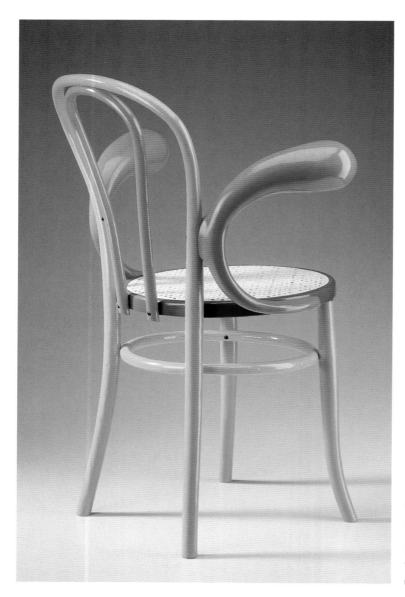

Garry Knox Bennett
Thonet | 2004

35 X 25 X 17 INCHES (88 X 64 X 43 CM)
Wood, fiberglass paint
PHOTO BY M. LEE FATHERREE

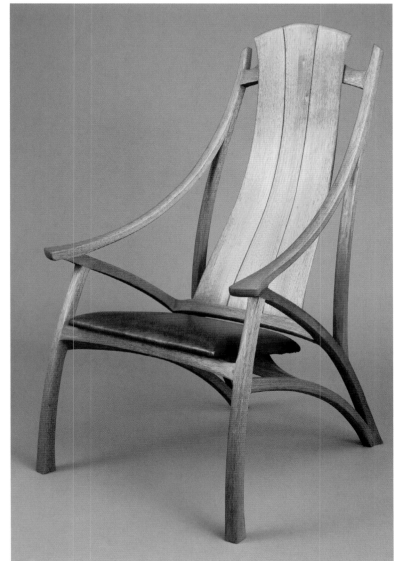

Donald Gray
Reading Chair | 2006

47 X 27 X 31 INCHES (118 X 69 X 78 CM)
Mahogany, leather
PHOTOS BY JOHN BIRCHARD

Curtis Buchanan

Velda's Chair | 2002

46 X 26 X 24 INCHES (117 X 66 X 61 CM)
Walnut, butternut, hickory, oil
PHOTO BY PETER MONTANTI

Curtis Buchanan

Bird Cage Side Chair | 1993

37 X 19 X 18 INCHES (94 X 48 X 46 CM)
Maple, oak, pine, milk paint. oil
PHOTO BY TOM PARDUE

Kaa chini *means "be seated" in Swahili. Inspiration for this design came from pictures of an African chief chair and from the upholstery technique called channeling.*

KERRY VESPER

Kerry Vesper
Kaa Chini | 2006

40 X 39 X 35 INCHES (100 X 98 X 88 CM)
Baltic birch, wenge

PHOTOS BY RON DERIEMACKER

Brian Boggs
Untitled | 2006

45 X 27 X 39 INCHES (113 X 68 X 98 CM)
Cherry, leather
PHOTO BY LOUIS CAHILL

Brian Boggs
Untitled | 2006

45 X 27 X 39 INCHES (113 X 68 X 98 CM)
Cherry, woven hickory bark
PHOTO BY LOUIS CAHILL

Thomas Dolese

Walnut Triangle Chair | 2006

32 X 30 X 29 INCHES (80 X 75 X 73 CM)

Walnut

PHOTO BY SCHERRER PHOTOGRAPHY

Johnny Whyte

Cockfight | 1998

42 X 57 X 23 INCHES (105 X 143 X 58 CM)
Claro walnut, Chinese elm burl
PHOTO BY ARTIST

> I always try to create movement in my forms. I feel it makes the piece more interesting and reconnects chair back to tree. MICHAEL GEORGE KARONIAS

Michael George Karonias

Autumn Harvest | 2006

60 X 22 X 20 INCHES (150 X 56 X 51 CM)
Mahogany, purpleheart, poplar
PHOTO BY JEANNE TAYLOR

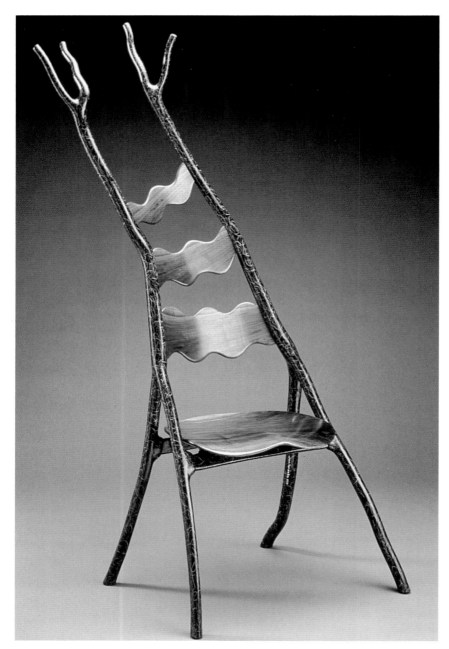

Jon Brooks

Dodge Hill | 1998

70 X 34 X 30 INCHES (175 X 85 X 75 CM)

Walnut, maple, color pencil, lacquer, acrylic, varnish

PHOTO BY DEAN POWELL

Graham Campbell

Rosinante | 2003

24 X 17 X 72 INCHES (61 X 43 X 180 CM)

Medium-density fiberboard, cherry, paint

PHOTO BY JOHN LUCAS

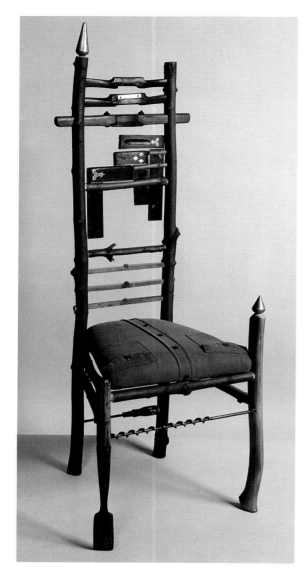

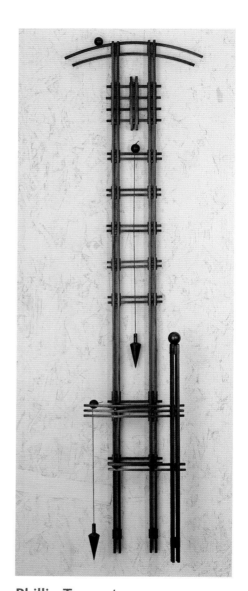

Daniel Mack
Tool Chair #3 | 1993

49 X 18 X 19 INCHES (123 X 46 X 48 CM)
Wood, tools
PHOTO BY BOBBY HANSSON

Phillip Tennant
Seat of Power | 2000

65 X 12 X 9 INCHES (163 X 31 X 23 CM)
Wood, graphite
PHOTO BY PATRICK BENNETT

Gord Peteran

Prosthetic | 2001

32 X 15 X 17 INCHES (80 X 38 X 43 CM)
Reclaimed wooden chair, brass
PHOTO BY ELAINE BRODIE

Kim Kelzer
Pair of Chairs | 2003

EACH: 34 X 24 X 24 INCHES (85 X 61 X 61 CM)
Mahogany, milk paint
PHOTO BY ARTIST

Kimberly Winkle

Children's Scarlet Blossom Faceted Chair | 2007

28 X 15 X 18 INCHES (71 X 38 X 46 CM)

Maple, poplar, graphite

PHOTO BY JOHN LUCAS

Clifton Monteith
Renwick Tall Chair | 2005

46 X 30 X 30 INCHES (115 X 75 X 75 CM)
Willow, aspen
PHOTOS BY JOHN WILLIAMS

Bobby Hansson

Celestial Throne for Nevelson

DIMENSIONS UNKNOWN
Wood
PHOTO BY ARTIST

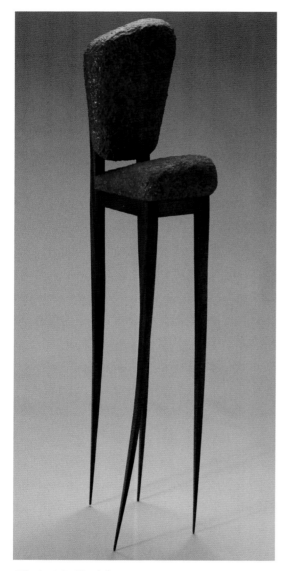

Trevor Toney
Sidechair | 2004

39 X 16 X 19 INCHES (96 X 41 X 48 CM)
Walnut
PHOTO BY ARTIST

Chris M. Todd
TippyToes | 2006

57 X 10 X 13 INCHES (143 X 25 X 33 CM)
Mahogany, foam, paper pulp, resin
PHOTO BY EDEN REINER

Jacob Cress

OOPS! | 1991–2002

40 X 20 X 18 INCHES (100 X 50 X 46 CM)

Walnut

PHOTO BY BOB VAUGHAN

Kristina Madsen

Dining Chair | 1994

38 X 20 X 19 INCHES (95 X 51 X 48 CM)

Dyed imbuya, silk

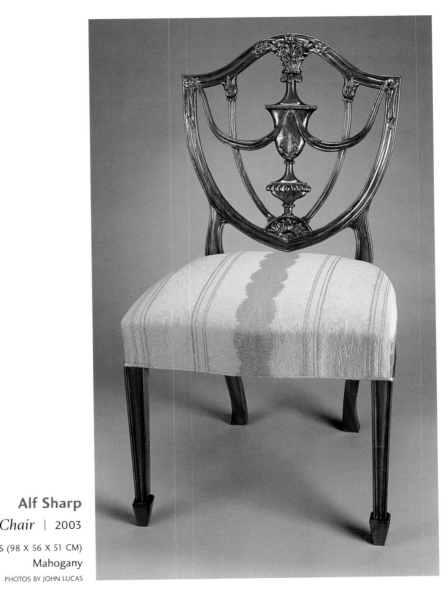

Alf Sharp

Shield-Back Chair | 2003

39 X 22 X 20 INCHES (98 X 56 X 51 CM)
Mahogany
PHOTOS BY JOHN LUCAS

William Thomas

New York–Style Federal Side Chair | 2000

36 X 21 X 21 INCHES (92 X 53 X 53 CM)
Mahogany, holly inlays, ash
PHOTO BY DEAN POWELL

William Thomas

Hepplewhite-Style Chair | 1999

35 X 21 X 22 INCHES (89 X 53 X 56 CM)
Cherry, birch inlays, silk
PHOTO BY DEAN POWELL

Gregg Lipton

Gazelle Chair | 1992

45 X 19 X 21 INCHES (114 X 48 X 53 CM)
Cherry, tiger maple
PHOTO BY STRETCH TUEMMLER

Laney K. Oxman

Victorian Telephone Settee | late 1990s

34 X 76 X 38 INCHES (85 X 190 X 95 CM)

Wood, clay, fabric, paint

PHOTO BY PHOTO WORKS, LEESBURG, VA

This chair is designed with wedged-through half-dovetails and wedged-through tenons. It is 'knock-down' and does not require glue or hardware in its construction or integrity.

BARRY DAGGETT

Barry Daggett

9-Piece Chair | 1996

42 X 26 X 23 INCHES (105 X 65 X 58 CM)
White oak, nylon string
PHOTO BY ARTIST

Chris Hoke
Al Tuttle

Variation on Adirondack Chair with Matching Table | 2007

42 X 38 X 34 INCHES (105 X 95 X 85 CM)
Willow
PHOTO BY AL TUTTLE

Takanobu Sekito

Untitled | 2006

DIMENSIONS UNKNOWN

Ash, paper cord

PHOTOS BY CORY ROBINSON AND PHIL TENNANT

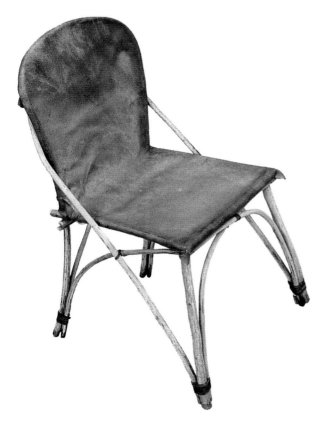

Brad Smith
Mower Handle Chair | 2007

35 X 16 X 20 INCHES (88 X 41 X 51 CM)
Cherry, reclaimed barn siding, reel mower handle
PHOTO BY ARTIST

Tor Faegre
Rawhide & Willow Chair | 2002

40 X 18 X 22 INCHES (100 X 46 X 56 CM)
Rawhide, peeled willow
PHOTO BY ARTIST

Miles Epstein

SF Wheel Chair | 2006

52 X 26 X 28 INCHES (130 X 65 X 70 CM)

Wine corks, cardboard, scrap copper, leather

PHOTOS BY ARTIST

Kenton Hall

Settee | 1987

32 X 50 X 24 INCHES (80 X 125 X 60 CM)

Walnut, oak, pine, milk paint

PHOTO BY DEAN POWELL

Buckthorn is an invasive tree in the Midwest and everyone wants to get rid of it. I made this chair to show off its one good quality, a glowing orange heartwood. TOR FAEGRE

Tor Faegre
Buckthorn Chair | 2006

36 X 30 X 24 INCHES (90 X 75 X 61 CM)
Buckthorn, rawhide
PHOTO BY ARTIST

Lee A. Schuette

Teakwood Shaker Rocker | 2003

41 X 20 X 24 INCHES (103 X 51 X 61 CM)
Teak, aluminum, webbing
PHOTO BY DOUG PRINCE

Lee A. Schuette

High Tech Shaker Side Chair | 1998

43 X 20 X 19 INCHES (108 X 51 X 48 CM)
Purpleheart, aluminum, tennis racket string
PHOTO BY DOUG PRINCE/UNH PHOTO SERVICE

Ted Hukill

Untitled | 2007

31 X 23 X 19 INCHES (78 X 58 X 48 CM)

Ash

PHOTO BY JIM DUGAN

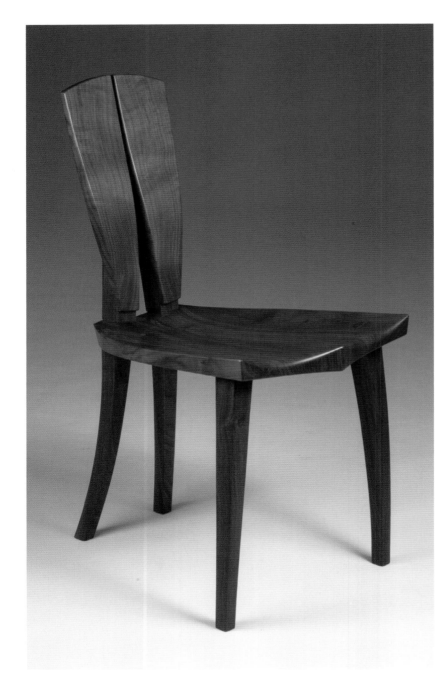

Paul Lynch
Untitled | 2004

32 X 18 X 17 INCHES (80 X 46 X 43 CM)
Claro walnut
PHOTO BY ARTIST

Paul M. Minniti

Mind Your Manners | 1998

41 X 19 X 20 INCHES (103 X 48 X 51 CM)
Cherry, fabric
PHOTO BY AUTHOR

Aaron Fedarko

Amigo Chair | 2007

40 X 19 X 17 INCHES (100 X 48 X 43 CM)
Cherry, black leather
PHOTO BY JIM DUGAN

Tai Lake

Watchers Chairs | 2001

EACH: 39 X 22 X 24 INCHES (98 X 56 X 61 CM)

Hawaiian koa

PHOTO BY ARTIST

Nathan Hunter

Gazelle Dining Chair | 2005

EACH: 38 X 18 X 22 INCHES (95 X 16 X 56 CM)
Walnut, curly maple, ebony, sapele, yellowheart
PHOTOS BY SPECTRUM STUDIO

Steve Butler

Transitional Limbo | 2003

18 X 20 X 20 INCHES (46 X 51 X 51 CM)
Poplar, cherry, photo transfers, ceramic tile, milk paint
PHOTO BY ARTIST

Brad Johns

Soft Landing | 2005

31 X 18 X 26 INCHES (78 X 46 X 66 CM)
Spanish cedar, padauk
PHOTO BY LARRY STANLEY

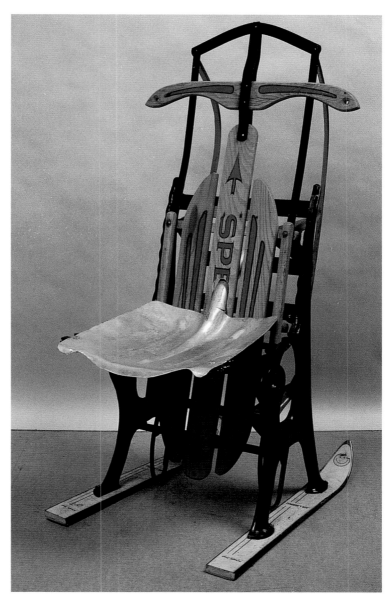

Bobby Hansson

*Throne for Snow Queen
Susan Butcher* | 1987

DIMENSIONS UNKNOWN
Sled, ski, snow shovel
PHOTO BY ARTIST

Sylvie Rosenthal

700 Miles Home | 2001

61 X 30 X 38 INCHES (153 X 75 X 95 CM)
Steel
PHOTO BY ARTIST

Dean Pulver

Untitled | 2004

32 X 26 X 23 INCHES (80 X 65 X 58 CM)
Dyed walnut
PHOTO BY PAT POLLARD

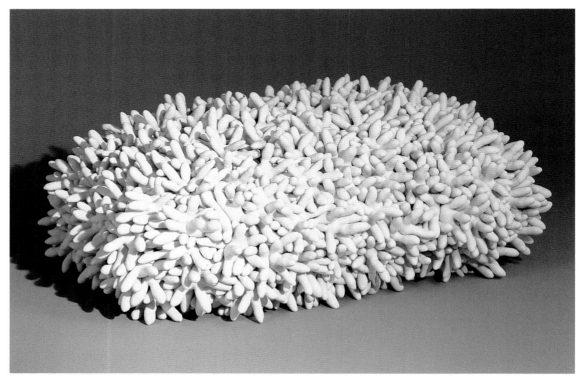

Rosario Mercado
Nature | 2005

18 X 28 X 42 INCHES (46 X 71 X 105 CM)
Latex gloves, polyester fiberfill
PHOTOS BY ARTIST

Shlomit Kalian Simchaev

Woven Chair | 2007

19 X 14 X 14 INCHES (48 X 36 X 36 CM)

Iron, metal net, plastic

PHOTOS BY REUVEN MARTON

Nikolai Moderbacher
2 x 4 Strapped | 2006

50 X 41 X 130 INCHES (125 X 103 X 325 CM)
Wood, strapping
PHOTOS BY ARTIST

> *Catawampus is a chair sculpture that is a self-portrait. The chair, like myself, is strong and well crafted, but is also warped and skewed, not perfect.*
>
> PHILLIP TENNANT

Phillip Tennant

Catawampus | 2002

62 X 14 X 16 INCHES (155 X 36 X 41 CM)
Bleached ash, brass plumb-bob, cord

PHOTO BY PATRICK BENNETT

Cameron Van Dyke
Wave | 2006

24 X 192 X 48 INCHES (60 X 480 X 120 CM)
Fiberglass, gel coat

Vincent Robles

Trestle Chair #1 | 2006

36 X 30 X 13 INCHES (90 X 75 X 33 CM)
Dyed ash
PHOTO BY LARRY STANLEY

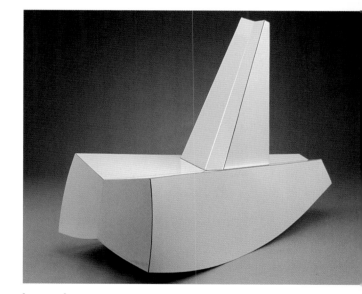

Isaac Arms

Little Rocker | 2005

40 X 20 X 50 INCHES (100 X 50 X 125 CM)
Steel, powder coating
PHOTO BY BILL LEMKE

Mitch Ryerson

Union Square Chairs | 2006

39 X 64 X 32 INCHES (98 X 160 X 80 CM)

Marine plywood, copper, epoxy

PHOTO BY ARTIST

This garden chair was fabricated by welding together nearly 1,000 individual 2-inch stainless steel washers, without any use of a mold, jig, or fixture. PETER DIEPENBROCK

Peter Diepenbrock

Washer Chair #3 | 2005

48 X 48 X 48 INCHES (120 X 120 X 120 CM)

Stainless steel

PHOTOS BY ARTIST

Tom Loeser

Cinch | 2007

48 X 60 X 60 INCHES (120 X 150 X 150 CM)

Industrial felt, steel strapping

PHOTO BY ARTIST

About the Juror

Craig Nutt has more than 35 years of experience as a studio furniture maker and sculptor. His vegetable-inspired work is included in numerous collections, including the Smithsonian's American Art Museum, the High Museum of Art in Atlanta, Hartsfield-Jackson Atlanta International Airport, the Birmingham Museum of Art, the Huntsville Museum of Art, the Mobile Museum of Art, and the Tennessee State Museum.

Craig was a founder and board member of the Furniture Society, an international organization dedicated to advancing the art of furniture making; he currently serves on the society's advisory board. He has been a board member of numerous other arts organizations, including the Alabama Crafts Council and the Southeast Regional Assembly of the American Craft Council. He currently serves on the Artists' Council of the Frist Center for the Visual Arts in Nashville, Tennessee, and the board of Tennesseans for the Arts.

Craig served as Interim Director of the Tennessee Association of Craft Artists in 2006, and he is currently Director of Programs for the Craft Emergency Relief Fund (CERF), a national organization that provides assistance to craft artists who have suffered career-threatening emergencies. He is a frequent panelist and juror for craft shows and fellowship programs, and he writes and lectures occasionally on the topics of art, furniture, and craft.

Contributing Artists